COMMUNITY LINK

GW01099415

ISH 04/24

07 OCT 2024

SURREY
COUNTY COUNCIL

Overdue items may incur charges as published in the current Schedule of Charges.

L21

Edna Johnson Wilson

Published by

GENERAL STORE PUBLISHING HOUSE

499 O'Brien Rd., Box 415, Renfrew, Ontario, Canada K7V 4A6
Telephone (613) 432-7697 or 1-800-465-6072
www.gsph.com

ISBN 1-897113-22-6
Printed and bound in Canada

Cover design, formatting and printing by
Custom Printers of Renfrew Ltd.

No part of this book may be reproduced, stored in a retrieval system or transmitted in any form or by any means, without the prior written permission of the publisher or, in case of photocopying or other reprographic copying, a licence from Access Copyright (Canadian Copyright Licensing Agency), 1 Yonge Street, Suite 1900, Toronto, Ontario, M5E 1E5.

Library and Archives Canada Cataloguing in Publication Data

Wilson, Edna M., 1921–
    Letters from London : 1944–1945 / Edna M. Wilson.

ISBN 1-897113-22-6

    1. Wilson, Edna M., 1921–. 2. London (England)--History--Bombardment,1940-1945--Personal narratives, Canadian. 3. World War,1939–1945--Personal narratives, Canadian. 4. Canada. Royal Canadian Air Force--Biography. 5. Canadians--England--London--Biography. I. Title.

D811.W57 2005   940.54'2121'092   C2005-905782-3

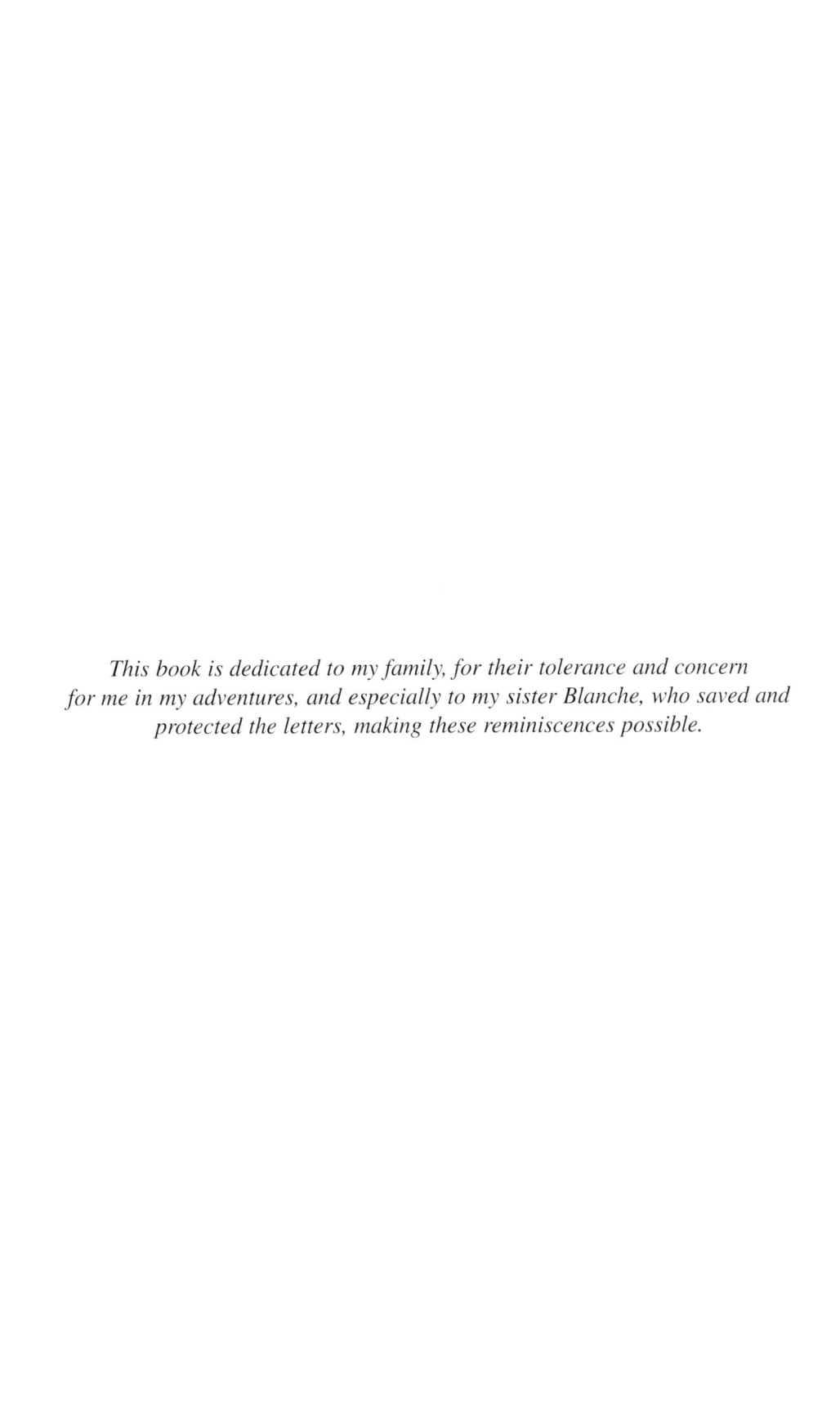

This book is dedicated to my family, for their tolerance and concern for me in my adventures, and especially to my sister Blanche, who saved and protected the letters, making these reminiscences possible.

Foreword

How wonderful that Edna Wilson's letters, sent home from London during World War II, have survived to this day! And how generous it is for her to have had them reproduced for our enjoyment. Because these letters were written as the action occurred, and her story is not simply based on reminiscences, they have the effect of transporting one backward as in a time machine.

For me, that means revisiting the envy felt by those of us in the RCAF (Women's Division) who were serving in Canada, but would have accepted at a minute's notice, as Edna did, an opportunity to go overseas. As Senior Officer in Charge of RCAF (WD) Supplies for Canada and Overseas, for instance, my position was classed as "essential" at Headquarters (Ottawa), and no amount of persuasion on my part could change that fact.

For other women, it will bring back memories of their own tour of duty in Canada or overseas: in the Canadian Women's Auxiliary Air Force (CWAAF), first formed in 1941 and subsequently renamed the RCAF Women's Division (WDs); in the Canadian Women's Army Corps (CWACs), which started recruiting a few weeks later; or in the Royal Canadian Navy, which did not begin recruiting women (WRENS) until late 1942.

And for those who were not involved in World War II, especially grandchildren and great-grandchildren, this story will provide a stark illustration of the changes that have taken place in the sixty years since the letters were written. Changes in communication, from the days when what is now referred to as "snail mail" was the only viable way for service people overseas to keep in touch with faraway family. Its delivery depended on the safe arrival of ships and planes that were under constant threat of being destroyed. Changes in technology, from the days—before photocopiers or computers—when shorthand, typewriters and carbon paper were basic tools, and stenographers were vital to any transfer of information.

But most strikingly, changes that have taken place in the role of women. Our enlistment for military service during World War II opened up new avenues for us. After the war, for the most part, our choice became to follow a career or to marry and bring up a family. Many of those who made the family choice conveyed to their daughters the sense of responsibility and increased spheres of action they had enjoyed during the war, so that generations of young women who followed and went on to higher education wanted a career and a family. And it goes without saying that the mores and attitudes that are evident in Edna's letters, and the comradeship and fun enjoyed by the Canadians in England, marked what really was an age of innocence.

We are grateful to Edna for sharing details of this brief period of her life. Her candour and her dry sense of humour add a tang to the telling. Because these were letters home, they obviously played down the daily bombings and fear of attacks, and the "loss in action" of comrades and school classmates that was common to us all.

Her contemporaries can relate to the historical notes that are added, and on the occasions when we are privileged to get together, reminiscences from that time so long ago make us feel as if those wartime experiences happened only yesterday.

We're all getting "up there" in years, but that will not stop us from having a sixty-fifth reunion of RCAF (WD)s in Winnipeg in June 2006!

Norma E. Walmsley, OC
Wakefield, Quebec
July 2005

Introduction

I have been a tick in the pendulum of history, and by noting these slight events, this tick might join with others to make a pattern for the future.

My interest has always been in airplanes in a minor way. In 1926, when I was five years old, the family's Sunday afternoon was a drive to Moose Jaw airport to watch some flimsy-looking planes take off and land. These were mainly JN4—Jennys—that had a history of their own. They were veterans of World War I. These in particular had not been over the battlefields, but were made-in-Canada war surplus. My father had three of these, just before my time, bought to invest in barnstorming. Pilots would fly around the country, land on a farm near a town, and take adventurous people for a thrilling ride for pay—not a long-lasting business. As far as I know, my father never flew the planes, but one of the pilots had been a lieutenant in the Flying Corps. See the movie *The Great Waldo Pepper* for an idea of what this fad was all about.

Between then and September 3, 1939, when world war was declared again, there were immeasurable advances in air transportation. On that particular Sunday, some of my family and friends went to Regina Beach to spend the afternoon by the lake. There was a refreshment stand with a juke box, and my brother laid out the rule that when his friends heard "Begin the Beguine" three times, they should be ready to leave. Thus, "Begin the Beguine" became a war song to me.

By 1942, I was, at twenty, old enough to enlist, and did so in the Air Force. I harboured no illusions that the men would allow women near airplanes, but the proximity was enough to tempt me.

I arrived at Manning Pool on Jarvis Street in Toronto at the end of May 1942. The basic training took one month—inoculation shots, how and who to salute, how to tie a tie, and the proper wearing of the issued uniform and assorted clothing. A second month was needed to learn clerical business, forms, procedures, etc. This was early enough in the new service that women in uniform were looked on with some suspicion.

Finally, I was posted to a station, No. 1 Bombing and Gunnery School, Jarvis, Ontario, which was just what it said—bombing and gunnery from the air. There were 360 British Commonwealth Air Training Plan schools built in Canada, and all air crew and technicians enrolled in the RAF and RCAF were trained here. Each station had up to five hangars, a headquarters building, a hospital, mess halls, barracks, a recreation building, and incidental buildings. An enormous staff was required to support these schools—training, maintenance, support, administration—and to fly and maintain the aircraft.

Canada's total male enlistment in the RCAF was 213,016, and in the Women's Division, 16,666.

It was not too hard to get used to living in a dormitory, although there was no room for personal "gee-gaws" or unmilitary clothing. The supervision was very like a convent. Most worked from eight to five for twelve days, then had two days off to look for some civilian life. I used to go into Hamilton and stay in a hotel for food and sleep.

I worked in the office of the maintenance hangar, typing situation reports and orders, and in the materiel office, busy with clothing for the passing classes of airmen. Life was almost completely on the station—living, work, and recreation. Holidays were observed, and tragedies happened.

Two years passed with two or three vacations home in Saskatchewan. What fun to travel by train halfway across Canada for $10.

Finally, the opening that every WD who enlisted for adventure was waiting for—an overseas draft.

When I heard about it I was up to HQ quick as a wink to assure the WD officer that I was fitted for an overseas posting, and deserved it. No mention was made of where overseas, but I was ready. I got someone to take my clearance around, a piece of paper that each applicable section—library, canteen, stores, etc.—had to sign to guarantee that I was not in debt to them.

Then I had just the regulation two weeks' embarkation leave. Off to Saskatchewan to the tsk! tsk! of my family.

Embarkation formalities were done at the depot at Lachine, Quebec. Missing inoculations were quickly supplied, clothing lists were brought up to date, and gas masks were tried out in a gas chamber (wooden hut with a door at each end). This is where I met my friend and roommate for the next year and half, Doris Johnson from Toronto, from being together in the always alphabetical line-ups. When all fifty of us were ready, off we went by train straight to the dock at Halifax.

The *Empress of Scotland* (formerly *Empress of Japan*) was loading troops. We struggled with our kit bags up the gangway, where an occasional soldier stepped forward to help. There were many ships in harbour, but it appeared that we were going alone—not in a convoy. We were on the luxury A deck, but with six bunks in what had been a single cabin and a bathroom across the hall. During the five-day trip I helped with the clerical work and the passenger lists that tried to keep track of the thousands on board from all services. Our desk and chairs were packing cases of cigarettes, which gradually disappeared as they were distributed. Rumour went around that our ship had been reported sunk by U-boats in the home-town press. Then rumour went around that this rumour went around every troop ship.

We arrived at Gourouk in northern Scotland in evening twilight, 11 p.m. by the clock. By train, after a day stopover at an RAF station in Gloucestershire, we got to London. This was our posting, Air Force Headquarters.

We had a quick information meeting—no barracks, no messes, no parades—so as to avoid concentrating any number of troops, before we were allotted bunks in some kind of dormitory. But the continuous noise of aircraft flying overhead made it impossible to sleep. How did London people stand this, we wondered, before seeing a newspaper headline the next morning. The invasion was on. It was June 6, 1944.

We were given a short conducted tour on how to travel by bus and underground, as well as several addresses of rooming houses. Doris and I picked one in Kensington, an old brick row house. We took the room down the stairs from the door, but at ground level, with window doors to an open court. The tenants were all Canadian military. We found our way to work, the Salvation Army hostel, the reasonable local restaurant, and our "local"—the Crown and Sceptre.

After a few days, a different-sounding aircraft motor came overhead, followed quickly by a large explosion. After a day of media speculation the government announced that these were unmanned small craft, whose sole purpose was to deliver the ton of explosive they carried. They were very effective. They could be heard approaching day or night, but seemed to head in randomly. Due to a flaw in their automatic controls, they often coasted in and circled, rather than drop as intended. My roommate claimed that one chased her around the block. This caused the longest alert ever sounded over London—two days. We found out that the military knew from intelligence that some super weapon was planned by the Germans for south England. They called it *Vergeltungswaffe* 1 (retaliation), or V1.

There seemed to be an anti-aircraft gun at one end of our street and a barrage balloon at the other. After a few days the gun disappeared, and we were told it was moved to the coast with all the rest.

Because at work we were connected to the Ministry of Aircraft Production alarm system, we continued with our duties during alarms. This gave us a false sense of security, as by the time we received the imminent danger signal, the buzz bomb had gone over or never appeared. We also criss-crossed our windows with tape, because when the glass imploded, it broke into long, knife-like splinters. Luckily, our windows remained intact.

It was a different story at home. One day we arrived home after work to find our front door blown out. Down to our room, we found our windows blown in. A flying bomb had pretty well destroyed a house just across the court from us. After a few days it got pretty nerve-wracking, and Doris was especially nervous. It was marvellous to me how the English stood it after years of regular bombing. The government asked anyone who could to leave London, and we were notified to be ready to leave on twenty-four hours' notice. The notice never came.

Some people who lived in the country took in London workers for a weekend respite. I was lucky enough to go to a family in Cambridge.

The powers-that-be estimated ten per cent casualties for Headquarters, not knowing yet the form of attack they were expecting. Our WD draft was fifty. Headquarters staff was 500. Gladly, their speculation was wrong, and the only headquarters person I know of who was killed was a civilian and her mother.

The launching site for the buzz bombs was found and bombarded, and fighter planes and special artillery stopped all but 5,600 out of 8,000 that were sent over.

Late in the summer we heard tremendous bangs that, unlike the V1, had no engine sounds to warn of their arrival. After these happened, it was announced that these were the V2s, a weapon that military specialists had expected before the V1 had arrived. The V2 was a true rocket with one ton of explosive. It was launched miles high and came down at terrific speed, giving it great impact force. There was no sound—if you heard it that was the last thing you heard. The launching site and storage sites were found and bombed before ground troops got to them.

Things were winding down, and a different spirit began to emerge in London. Rationing still continued, but bomb damage was being cleared.

Through the winter we listened to the news of the Allied forces progressing across Europe. London seemed to be the location of choice for servicemen to spend leaves, now that they were being granted. Staff in London had only short leaves. I spent a week at Balliol College, Oxford, attending special lectures and social events. There I met a Canadian soldier from Borden, near Aldershot, who afterwards came to London to visit me.

Finally, it was announced that total surrender was signed on May 7, and Victory Day would be observed May 8, with a holiday on May 9 to recover. On Tuesday evening three of us from the house decided to go downtown. We got only as far as Piccadilly, and had to walk up the Mall with thousands of Londoners celebrating. We were more or less washed into the area in front of Buckingham Palace. I found out after that there were one million people in that area. Royalty, family, and Churchill came out on the balcony repeatedly. To be part of this crowd was an indescribable feeling.

After a long evening we started home but, of course, with this concentration of people in the West End, no transportation was running. I figure it was five miles from the Palace to Holland Road, on hot pavement with only one chance at warm lemonade. Our own local was open for celebration, and a cool pint helped our feet.

The Emperor of Japan conceded his armies in early August, and the war was over.

Although an anticlimax, work continued in our office, but armed forces were being organized for rehabilitation.

My number came up in December. As a last farewell from England, we were gathered in every hotel in Brighton. Finally to Southampton to the

Queen Elizabeth, along with 10,000 troops. They could only serve us two meals a day, but we enthused on white bread and good food.

Five days later we docked in New Jersey, then they loaded 25 trains—ours to Montreal, then cross-Canada by CPR troop train. It arrived in Vancouver a whole day late, but the media had been keeping track of us. At every station along the way we were cheered. I proceeded to pick up a civilian life—not quite as I had planned. I married the soldier I had met at Oxford and went to live in Ottawa.

I kept up an interest in veterans and volunteered at the War Museum. In 1994, the fiftieth anniversary of the D-Day invasion, different government departments organized a grand weekend celebration honouring veterans of the invasion. My connection was tenuous (London, June 6, 1944), but I was allowed to take part. Starting at Lansdowne Park, war vehicles and trucks filled with troops passed the length of Bank Street. There had been publicity, but I was stunned that the street was lined with people, waving and shouting, "Thank you." It was touching and brought us to tears—one of my greatest experiences.

On looking back on my service years, especially as I read over the letters I wrote home from London, I remember many small incidents and great people. Life in wartime London was not a unique experience, but it was interesting.

Edna M. (Johnson) Wilson
RCAF (WD) W304478

CANADIAN LEGION  **STATION CHAPLAIN (P)**
No. 1 Y DEPOT R.C.A.F.
LACHINE, P.Q.

WAR SERVICES

....194......

Dear Mrs. Johnson,

Just a note to say that Edna is on her way. She attended church before leaving and asked me to send you her love.

It may be several weeks before you hear from her so don't worry. May God watch between you and her while you are parted one from another.

Sincerely yours,

(G.S. Tanton)

PLEASE USE BOTH SIDES

W304478
Johnson E. M.
RCAF (WD)

Somewhere—Period
Time—8:30

Dear Mom & Dad:

I am starting this at sea so I can mail it when I arrive so it won't be so long till you get a letter after my cable.

We were sure rushed through Lachine but when I saw it I didn't tell you so you won't worry. I think Kenny would catch on, though.

We have had a marvelous trip so far. We came first class from Lachine—sleepers and a dining car. We have been given officers' accommodation—we feel sorry for the poor mere sergeants. On the boat our accommodation is better than P.O.'s[1] and F.O.'s.[2] I am afraid we are getting spoiled and will be rudely awakened when we arrive.

The boat is the one that Kenny has been through, if you remember.

We eat in the officers' dining room and go in the officers' lounge—where we can get in. As usual there are all kinds of people who seem to know me, whom I stare at vaguely and say "Hello." However, I recognize them all as Jarvis-ites. If I knew the names of people who know mine I would know a lot.

Kenny was my brother, and he was married to Marg. I also had a sister Dorothy, in addition to Blanche. All were older than me. Marg wrote me occasionally, but Ken never did. Ken worked in advertising for B.C. Tree Fruits, but during the war, they loaned him to the government and he spent a while in the Maritimes looking after potato distribution. One weekend, when Ken was in the Maritimes, Blanche was in Washington, and I was at Jarvis, the three of us had a rendezvous in Hamilton with one of Blanche's friends. And I said that everybody had to go to Niagara Falls. Ken had been in the apple business, so we had to see the orchards. He wasn't impressed, compared to what he had been used to in the Okanagan.

Jarvis was the No. 1 Bombing and Gunnery School, near Hamilton, where I spent two years and, naturally, had a lot of friends there.

Later—evening

I went to church this morning. They had it in what must have been a kind of theatre, but which is now a mess and temporarily a church. There was a

---

[1] Pilot Officer
[2] Flying Officer

mob there—people stood at the back. I guess a lot of men going into action take life seriously.

It got rougher this afternoon. You would notice someone coming down the deck with his feet in one place and the rest of him 40 degrees ????. "Look at the damned fool," you thought, then look at yourself and discover you had a 45-degree list. It's fun, though. You find yourself flying upstairs and climbing like heck to get up a straight hall. I spend a lot of time just looking over the rail. I wish Dad could be here—he'd enjoy it.

Naturally there are a lot of officers aboard, and as there are about 50 men per girl the officers think they should have preference. Some of the girls said to heck with that, and went in the troops recreation room, but I guess the company was pretty rough and they don't go in any more. There are 4 P.O.'s from Jarvis here, and 1 L.A.C.[3] They drag up all their friends, and of course I don't do bad myself. To be friendly with I already know about 8 more P.O.'s and 5 sailors and 2 soldiers & 4 sergeants, and of course there are all the people you casually say hello to.

This is the third day out, and I haven't even been slightly sick. It really hasn't been rough enough for that. Yesterday I volunteered to work in the RCAF orderly room on board, mainly to shake an RAF P.O. who shadows me and jumps out from every corner. It kept me busy all day. I and a chap from Jarvis played a dirty trick on him last night, but he's still around today. It's funny—we had 3 boys who "joed" in the I&R[4] when I was there. I used to say, "Paint that floor good, boys, and I'll see you get your commission." They used to say they'd be glad to get overseas away from me because I was a slave driver, & I used to say I would be waiting for them there. Well, they're all on the boat—with commissions.

Next Day

Today has been foggy, rainy and windy. It is rougher but still not bad. I feel like an old salt. I worked in the Orderly Room this morning, got some air, then slept about 3 hours, then washed for supper. Afterwards we went out on deck. A lot of French Army Officers were holding a sing-song and they were good. Three of us in this cabin have been working in the Orderly Room and one of the warrant officers brings us coffee at night—about 11:30. They get it because they work late, so get extra for us. Have I told you yet we only eat twice a day? We have breakfast at 7:45 and dinner at 5:45. We can get biscuits and stuff at a canteen, but most of the time I forget to eat in between and don't miss it.

---

[3] Leading Aircraftman
[4] Issues and Receipts, a materials section.

Next Day

    I didn't go to the lounge last night as black-out wasn't till a little later than usual and I came to bed from the deck. We can't be out after the black-out goes into effect. They have a P.A. system with speakers all over the boat and an English voice regularly makes little announcements. This boat is breaking us in to England, if you get what I mean. It is cold again today.

    I guess I had better finish this today since I want to mail it on the boat. Luxury today—fresh water all day (in the taps, I mean)! We feel a little closer to the war now.

    I will write as soon as possible after we land to give you my first impressions of wherever we land (too bad I can't tell you—Uncle Dave would be interested—& it's not New Zealand).

    I hope my cable won't be delayed too long, because I suppose just about now you will be looking for a letter and cussing because you think I haven't written.

    So long for now,

    Love

    Teddy.

P.S. Did you get the suitcase alright? I haven't got Dorothy's address so can't write her.

Dear Blanche:

Guess I will start this now and mail it when we arrive (censored—destination a military secret). I know our destination by a number, but that is all. I have been working part time in the RCAF Orderly Room on board.

I never saw a place where so many rumours flew as on board a ship. Usually all of them are wrong so I don't believe any, which leaves me in the blissful state of ignorance.

When I phoned you I knew when we were leaving Lachine, but that didn't count for much. We had a dirty trip on the train but our accommodation was better than the sergeants.

This is starting the fifth day out and I haven't been sick. It hasn't been very rough,

My sister Blanche, when she worked in Washington

though. Just enough to let you know you are on a boat, and make you zig-zag down the corridors once in a while (I mean alley-ways).

Our sleeping accommodations are better than P.O.'s and F.O.'s, we eat in the officers' dining room and can go in the officers' lounge (if you have a shoe horn to get in the door.) I am having a swell time, no fooling. There are quite a few people here I know, and it certainly doesn't take long to get acquainted with others. I was surprised at the men who came up. "Well, hello, Johnny! What are you doing here?" I can't remember hardly any of their names, but I recognize them as former Jarvis-ites. It's a small world.

I wish I could tell you all about this but probably the censor will make paper dolls out of it now.

The sea air sure makes us sleep. In the day times we walk the deck, lean on the rail, sit in the sun (if any) and sleep. After black-out we sit (but mostly stand) in the lounge. We sure sleep at nights. The only thing I object to is losing an hour every night. It cuts down our sleeping time.

One rumour that went around decks was that the Canadian papers had reported our ship had been sunk. Then it went round that this rumour was heard on every troop ship!

Another Day

Stood on deck talking this morning, got cold and damp. On boat drill waiting for the inspecting party the officers and us had quite a little sing-song. They also dumped one guy into a garbage can. I really got thoroughly cold.

Worked in the Orderly Room this afternoon, went out for a while tonight and am now in bed. I have to finish this today, as I want to mail it aboard & won't have time to finish it tomorrow or the next day. It is staring to clear up, I think. I bet for about a week after I land I'll back for my life-belt before I move. You don't get very far without it before someone sends you back. Talked to a squadron leader last night from Regina. He knew the kids I went to school with, and married a girl that used to be in my room. We had a quite a gossip party.

We just have two meals a day, but I don't think I have lost any weight yet. I don't eat between meals either!

I have decided that what I suspicioned is true—the English can't cook. I'm not jumping to conclusions either—you can probably figure that one out. This ship is one that Kenny was through.

Yesterday standing in the spray and cold wind a chap from Trinidad showed me pictures of his family, and beaches, etc. around his home. It made me imagine I was warm, anyway. He is a marvellous singer—he sits and sings to me.

The WO[5] in the orderly room scrounges coffee from somewhere at night and brings some down to us every night about 11. Luxury.

I was complaining about all the salt on my face at boat drill and the P.O. next to me said "Maybe you're pickled and don't know it."

I really like the sea, though. It's wonderful. I would like to be on this run regularly, but the F.L. says "No women!" I like the sea, the work would be interesting, and I've had a good time. I even get along swell in rough weather. I've got used to dressing instead of undressing at night. We are supposed to be fully dressed at night so we put on our pyjamas, then slacks and sweater over them, our great coats on the foot of the bed and our water-wings & shoes handy beside the bed.

I have written to mom, too, and hope she isn't too long getting it. She would start wondering when she didn't get a letter this week.

You feel rather isolated out in the middle of the ocean, but you're not alone for long. One thing there isn't on a troop ship, and that's privacy, but that doesn't bother old service people like us.

Guess I'll sign off. I'll let you know as soon as I can what my first impressions of the promised land are.

Love,
Edna.

Couple of days Later

They wouldn't take a letter to the States on the boat, so I still have this. I am now at the reception centre for a couple of days or so.

[5] Warrant Officer

Several Days Later

I never did get this posted but will now. I haven't settled in work or a place to live yet but will shortly. We arrived in London yesterday and will be staying here. My address though is just
"R.C.A.F. Overseas."

Will write a letter right away to tell you about this queer town.

Love,

Edna.

My first night in England was not very promising. We were unloaded from the ship at Gourock and put on a train to an RAF station in Gloucestershire. Late at night, someone met us with a flashlight and took us to some kind of barracks. There we found on the bare cots biscuit mattresses—a first acquaintance for most of us. The mattresses were in three hard sections, which were piled on the bed during the day.

Early the next morning, someone opened the door and put on the light. "Time to get up!" was only responded to by grunts. In a short time, the door opened again and a very firm female sergeant-major confirmed that it was, indeed, time to get up.

As we paraded from place to place on the station, we were greeted with whistles and yells from some Canadian airmen. Then, after one more night with the RAF, we went on to London.

June 6/44.

Dear Mom & Dad:

I told you they were waiting for me to start the invasion!

I have been at a reception centre for a couple of days, but am now in London. Have seen a fair amount of it riding around in a truck yesterday. As for England, we saw quite a stretch of it from trains. It is lovely, and everything is just like midsummer. Eight of us went for a walk Sunday afternoon and saw some really ancient countryside.

The reception centre was for everyone, and when we arrived the boys practically mobbed us. Wherever we marched they lined the roads and shouted. Passing the parade square a whole parade turned around and rubbered. Such remarks as, "Gee it's good to hear a woman talk who can talk!" and "Don't mind me, I'm just looking at a white woman," and "What's No. 1 on the Hit Parade?" The Waafs[6] didn't like it very well. We distributed our attentions. About four guys in the canteen were slightly tipsy and talking to me I said I was from Sask. One guy jumped right up and hugged me right in the canteen.

[6] Women's Auxiliary Air Force

We have had a lot of laughs—trains and plumbing mainly. Our chief annoyances so far are the potatoes for breakfast and scarcity of bath tubs.

Just now we are staying in a club but are getting some place to live tomorrow. The girls live in 2's and 3's in rooms and apartments. They want them dispersed so their whole staff won't be bombed at once. I certainly don't want you to worry. London hasn't had a raid for a long while and, anyway, this particular building is charmed, because the building right next door is practically demolished and this one is not even touched.

I hope you got the cable. It shouldn't have been delayed too long because I paid enough for it.

I wish you could see Scotland. You're so fond of everything Scotch anyway. It is beautiful—far more lovely than England. The little fields are all divided by stone walls. The sheep have wool that hangs down to the round, and black faces. We even saw a lot of goats in one field. Up there, too, it is light until 11 o'clock. The Scotch people were very friendly, too.

We certainly see a lot of war equipment, if not war. We see a lot of results, too, and it makes us feel as if Canada didn't know there was a war on.

We stepped off the train yesterday here and there was a chap that Doris knew, and he and some friends wanted to take us out last night. Not bad, eh? We were too tired to go, though.

We haven't got settled either living or working, but will by Thursday.

I haven't written to Blanche yet—I hope you have let her know that I arrived.

I haven't started to look up people yet—will do it when I'm settled. Doris & I are going to live together. We've been together ever since Lachine.

Guess I will close this now as I have a couple of minutes to go to the Post Office.

My address is just
"R.C.A.F. Overseas."
So long,
Love
Teddy

A shocking welcome to London! Knowing nothing about the intended invasion and hearing aircraft all night long, we asked ourselves: How did people sleep? How could they stand it, night after night? The headlines in the morning newspapers provided the answer: D-Day.

London
June 12/44.

Dear Mom & Dad:

Well, at last we are settled in Ye Olde London—the town of pubs and outdoor plumbing.

I am settled at work—it is interesting in a way and boring in another. We have to parade every morning at 8:30. I can see right now I'm not going to lose any 10 pounds. We have three meals a day—quite a shock to my stomach after the boat—tea every afternoon and sometimes in the morning, and then again before we go to bed.

We stay quite a ways from work—about half an hour's ride on the tube (subway to you), and about 10 minutes' walk to the underground station, although we sometimes take the bus down to it. We are only in a temporary room—we move into another next week (in the same house). The landlady is very nice—she keeps popping in with tea. So far we have been eating breakfast here and dinner and supper either in the cafeteria in the office or at the Can. Legion. I don't know what we'd do without the Legion. They serve the best meals by a long way at only 1 and 6, which is one shilling and sixpence, which I never try to break down into Canadian money. I am rooming with Doris Johnson, whom I chummed with from Lachine on. We are going to cook for ourselves when we get established in our room with a gas ring.

In the short time I've been here I have already seen more of London than I can write about. We have had endless laughs.

Wednesday night I came out here, Thursday night we went to bed. Friday night we went to the Legion for supper, met a chap Doris used to know and popped around a corner for an ale. I was afraid ale would make me fat, but they all say the present variety certainly wouldn't. We came home & went to bed after getting soaking wet.

Saturday night we started to go to a dance, but the dance hall was full. Two English army officers suggested looking for another one, so we did, and it was full, too. We ended up walking up Charing Cross Road (which is no road, but a busy street) went into a pub, had one beer when the barkeeper shouted, "Time, Ladies & Gentlemen," which is to say he wants to close up. We walked up a little further and went into the darndest dive I ever hope to see. It was small, and full, but the civilians insisted on giving us their seats (the officers must have glared at them). One guy insisted on singing and the bartender leaped out and had him out the door before he knew what was happening.

Well, we had one drink and the barkeep shouted, "Time, Ladies and Gentlemen." What amused me was a great big scrawly sign right on the mirror above the bar saying, "No Ladies Toilet." Well, then we walked down Shaftesbury Avenue (more theatres than any other street in the world). The mob was awful, but we strolled down four abreast, arm in arm. We walked down as far as Leicester Square and Haymarket, then down Pall Mall and past St. James' Park right down the middle of the road—the cars go around you. We hung around the fence outside Buckingham Palace trying to distract the guard, but he wouldn't be distracted. Then the men hailed a car thinking it was a cab. It wasn't but he gave us a ride to the tube station anyway. They stop running at

12, so when you go out in London you go early and come home early. We parted for our various trains. They were a lot of fun, but they assured us they weren't typical officers because they had come through the ranks.

Sunday we have off. About 9:30 the landlady comes in with tea. I went back to sleep. About 12 she came in with lunch, so I got up & into my slacks. I washed my hair & put it up and then did my ironing. Then we sat and gabbed with a Canadian Army sergeant who stays here. We had tea. Then we went out for a walk down to the Thames River. We stopped in at a pub with a lovely beer garden, then came home, had tea again. Another army chap had shown up—I think he stays here, too, & we gabbed until 11 o'clock, then finally went to bed.

The things that still seem strange are the dark streets at night (although it is light until late because they are on double daylight saving), double-decker buses that look top heavy and always stop on the wrong side of the street, plumbing with the pipes all outside like an afterthought after building the house. The streets are impossible—crooked, some wide, some narrow, some change names every few blocks. They give addresses mainly by district—such as such-and-such a street in Earls Court, or Knightsbridge, or Hammersmith. Ours is Holland Road in Kensington High Street. However, we are not allowed to use our home address for correspondence, although we do use it within England.

I haven't got in touch with Tony yet. I haven't written to people I am supposed to yet. The Army is moving around terrifically.

I am sure glad I got here for the invasion. It doesn't affect our life, but first the excitement of it being so close is enough. Nice of them to wait for me, wasn't it?

There is somebody out of every military organization in the world here. You see everything. I have even seen French & Norwegian uniformed girls.

Guess I will close now and take a bath and to bed.

Haven't heard from you yet, but hope you got my mail. This is the third letter I have written you.

So long now,
Love
Teddy.

I guess you could call Mrs. MacLean our landlady, but it wasn't her house. She was the person hired to look after it. She had a big room on the ground floor, where we were, filled full of furniture—I don't know if it was from the house or was hers—and a little stove, and she sat by that stove and smoked all day. She also brought us tea, which I think was in our bargain.

We had a little gas ring in our room on which to cook, so we couldn't cook much even when we could get food. And there was only one bathroom for the fourteen of us. There might have been another toilet, on the top floor somewhere.

I always wondered where they got the thousands of yards of heavy black cotton used for the blackout curtains. Every window in a lighted room had to have them, and the local Air Raid Warden ensured they were used. Ironically, the windows of London reflected any little light—even moonlight—so the pilots could see the city despite the precautions we all took. They tried, but they couldn't hide London.

June 13/44.

Dear Blanche:

This is crummy weather for June, but yesterday was nice. They tell us they had summer before we came.

This is some town. We stay about half an hour's tube (spelled c-h-u-b-e) ride, and about 10 minutes walk to the underground station. We sometimes take the bus down to it. We are in a temporary room—we are waiting for a man to move out upstairs. We eat most of the time at the Canadian Legion— the best meals, the cheapest. Thank heavens for it. We are going to cook for ourselves when we get settled in our room. The landlady gives us our breakfast and always brings in tea at night. We have tea in the afternoon at the cafeteria here and sometimes in the morning. We sometimes eat dinner here, too; it is quite good.

I am rooming with the girl I chummed with from Lachine on—Doris Johnson. I have already seen more than I can write about. Conditions in London are about the best they have been since the war started—i.e. food, etc.—but they are expecting trouble. They haven't had an air raid for weeks, until last night there was an alert. The sirens sound just as mournful as they say. In fact there were two alerts and both woke me up. I don't know whether anything happened or not, though—I went back to sleep.

We are both just dying to go to a dance, so Saturday night we started out but found the hall full. Two English army officers offered to take us to another one, so we went. However, we found it full, too, so went for a walk down Charing Cross Road. We went into a pub of a hotel. Any pub that is in the basement they put up a sign "Dive," which scared us off at first but it turned out to be nice. We just had one ale when they wanted to close, so we went to another. It was tiny and painted blue on the outside. It was a dive, although it didn't have a sign. It was thick with smoke and people. We had one drink then it closed. Then we wandered down Shaftesbury Avenue, Leicester Square, Haymarket and Pall Mall to Buckingham Palace. It was getting late so the boys whistled at a car—it stopped and took us all to the Strand tube station where we got trains home. They stop running at 12 o'clock so you have to come home early.

Sunday I slept in, washed my hair, did my ironing, gabbed, and went for a walk with an army sergeant who stays in the house. I saw the Thames River— it just looks like an ordinary river to me.

Honestly, I wish you could see some of the things that just about kill us. The plumbing pipes on the outside of houses, the double-decker buses, no tops on the salt shakers, dark streets at night, the bath tubs you put tuppence in to get a bath, the maze of crooked streets that change names every few blocks, and the way we nearly get killed when we step off a curb because we always look the wrong way.

I see Sheila Bailey's address is not very far from where I live. I'm going to see if I can phone her. I haven't written to anybody yet.

The transportation system is tops, I think. So many people travel, but they always get there (in the city that is). There is an underground train not any further apart than 5 minutes, and you can get close to anywhere you want to go. Of course the buses are nice for sight-seeing.

I haven't written Kenny or Dorothy because I don't know their addresses.

We have no leave, and couldn't travel if we had, so I am going to see London now, then get a chance to see the rest of the country when we get leave.

Must close now. Hope to hear from you soon.

Love

Edna.

Doris always added another bag to the tea we bought from the cafeteria, as she said it was like "cricket's piddle."

There was an army sergeant, John "Mac" MacDonald, who lived upstairs. He came into our room one evening, threw his great-coat on the floor, and announced he was spending the night. Of course we protested, but were brought up short when a revolver fell out of the pocket.

Mac had vague information that some further horrors were impending for London. Our inner door opened up to a court that was surrounded by the houses around the block, with the only entry to this court through the houses.

He did spend the night, but we saw no paratroopers.

The further attacks came in the Fall in the V2, a terrible and destructive true rocket.

Mac was kind of the backbone of the house. He was married, from Little Pond, P.E.I., and worked in the Historical Section in the War Diaries. His boss was Colonel Stacey, who was quite an historian and author.

London
June 20

Dear Fat:[7]

Well, I'm going to see if my knees will stop knocking long enough to start a letter this noon hour.

People who never turned a hair in the big blitz are jittering right now. These winged bombs are ghostly things. They come over low and very fast—all of a sudden the motor stops and boom—they nose right down into the nearest building. One thing, you can see and hear them coming and they don't change course.

We were out the first night they came over. They have a little light on when the motor is going. It was a picked up in the searchlights and never moved in the gunfire. Thinking then that it was an aeroplane, that seemed odd to us. A few of them came over the next day and night and the gunfire was terrific—it kept up awake. They don't fire at them anymore now (here, at least); what gets through at the coast gets through & that's all. One night a hospital down the street from us was hit. Night before last one hit just about 3 blocks away. Yesterday we had a bad day, but our nerves are fine today. When we got to work yesterday morning we discovered a building right behind ours had been hit just at 7 o'clock. It was still smoking and people were digging—they were still digging at noon. The limit of destruction seems to be one fair-sized building and windows blown out for about a block around. Well we have a system of bells in the building, which are rung for imminent danger, and we can go to the shelter if we want. They rang all morning but nobody felt like walking down 6 flights when the alarm is on and off. At noon we were eating dinner in the cafeteria when a girl said, "There goes one." One whizzed by, then crash!—it landed somewhere in Piccadilly and the smoke just poured up—that gave us a turn.

Last night Mac said he'd take us down the street to see the day before's damage. We looked at it—it was a church, and at the surrounding windowless buildings. We walked a ways when we heard one coming—it's hard to tell them from a plane. Well, it passed and crashed a little ways over. We each grabbed one of his hands, shaking like Kate Smith[8] or an aspen leaf and made him bring us home. I'm not really scared—just sensibly cautious. The suspense is in hearing it coming and wondering just when the motor is going to stop. Well enough of that—I sure wouldn't have missed it for anything.

Thursday night Doris and I went to the Beaver Club.[9] They had a dance until 10 o'clock. We went out with two guys afterwards but, of course, have to start home before 12. We just got to the door when the guns started going. Flak is pretty at night—it glows red and looks just like fireworks.

---

[7] An unkind, although sisterly nickname for Blanche.
[8] Kate Smith (1907–86) was one of the most popular singers of the time and is perhaps best-known for making famous the Irving Berlin song, "God Bless America."
[9] The Beaver Club was the Canadian club in London.

Friday night we went to bed. Friday I got moved to another job temporarily. The W/C sent me out on an errand, which included a bus trip past the Houses of Parliament, Westminister Abbey, Big Ben and the Thames River—very nice. Went to one of these places where you make out a pass but the escort doesn't lose sight of you anyway. Saturday afternoon we went to see "The Student Prince" at the Stoll Theatre. It was quite good.

Sunday we slept until noon and sat out in the sun all afternoon, did our ironing, etc.

We have been cooking for ourselves at night. Groceries aren't awfully expensive, but clothes are. Blouses 3£, shoes 6£—can you feature it?

I wrote to mom yesterday—I got 2 letters from her and two from you—all forwarded from Lachine. Also got cute cards from Minnie and Joyce, a note about my bond from the bank, ditto from A.F.H.Q., and also a bulletin from the Book of the Month Club.

Since we had no leave I still have my 20£, but I saw Scotland anyway. They are starting to give us 48's.[10] One a month I suppose. We now get Sat afternoon and Sunday off.

[Paper stained] . . . nylon stocking situation? I assigned Mom $10 a month to buy stuff for me, so let her know whatever you spend on me.

No comment on your week-end with Herbie.

There is an awful lot to say about England and Englishmen, but I have a hunch my pen is almost dry. You can have a bed that looks like "George Washington Slept There" if you like.

We are going to try to go to Albert Hall some night. It is out this way some place and concerts only cost 2 shillings. Re your remarks about the money—maybe I have trouble with arithmetic, but I can always figure out money. I don't always let the clerk figure it out, either. My secret is—don't compare it with Canadian. If you do stuff will sound so expensive you won't buy it.

Mac (the Can. Army Sgt.) who lives here is taking us to see London proper on Sunday. It hasn't been touched by bombs, I don't [paper stained] . . . I had a camera. Now we can get out and will be able to see a bit of country-side too.

Well, I guess this is enough. I just heard yesterday that Saskatchewan went C.C.F. and it floored me. C.C.F.'ers get out to vote—I think that's it. Anyway, the gang over here are going to run Canada their own way when they get back.

So long for now,
Love
Edna.
W304478
Johnson E. M.
R.C.A.F. Overseas.

[10] A forty-eight-hour leave.

Historical Note: On June 15, 1944, the Co-operative Commonwealth Federation Party, with Tommy Douglas as its leader, overthrew the governing Liberals in Saskatchewan to become the first socialist government elected anywhere in North America. The CCF won forty-seven of fifty-two seats in the legislature and more than half of the popular vote. This, despite a very negative campaign by the governing Liberals, who accused Douglas of being a communist.

June 25/44.

Dear Mom & Dad:

I hope you have had some mail from me by this time. I got two letters from you last week forwarded from Lachine. If you wrote once a week I should have another one soon.

We have been tired this week (they told us when we came we would be tired about a month, so we should soon feel normal). Besides that, we didn't like the idea much of going out at night with all these doodle-bugs around, so we stayed in all week, except for little jaunts around our district with Mac, but we always came in about 9.

Saturday night Doris and I went to a dance at Covent Gardens. It is a grand dance hall—super deluxe. The place was full of Americans. We had a nice time. The dance ended at a quarter to 11, we were home by 11:30....

Guess I will close this now as I want to be sure it gets away.

If you haven't sent a parcel yet, how about sending us a small table clock? We finally got our second kit bag.

Well, so long for now,

Love,

Teddy.

Historical Note: The V1, commonly referred to as "buzz bombs," "doodlebugs," or "ying bombs," was one of Nazi Germany's last serious attempts to wipe out London. Launched from ramps along the coasts of Belgium and France, and eventually Holland, they could fly at speeds estimated between 300 to 450 miles per hour, meaning it would take them about twenty-five minutes to reach London. They were programmed to dive suddenly to the ground from a flying height of 2,000 feet after the small propeller attached to the nose had made a specific number of revolutions. While head and tail winds affected their accuracy, they did inflict terrible psychological damage on the British public—Hitler's primary goal. This to an already weary populace who had just come through the Blitz.

The first doodlebug hit London on June 13, 1944, a week after D-Day. By the end of the month they averaged around fifty a day. They had an odd "putt-putt" sound, which alerted people to their impending approach, and Londoners learned to almost ignore their presence—until the sound suddenly ceased. Then they had about fifteen seconds to find cover before the bomb exploded, causing extensive lateral damage. So, as long as they could hear that distinctive sound, they were safe.

June 30.

Dear Blanche:

Well, nothing much has happened this week—to me, I mean. This morning our doodle-bug that regularly chases us down the street at 10 minutes to 8 didn't make an appearance. I guess they were holding them all until noon hour—sure sounded like it, anyway. We have hardly gone out at night because things are little rough. They say it's marvellous downtown—the shows aren't crowded, and you can even get a taxi.

We did our ironing, and went out just around the district a couple of nights last week.

Saturday night we went to a dance at Covent Gardens—a lovely ballroom. We had a nice time; there were a slew of Americans there. Sunday, Mac and I and Doris and one of the Yanks went sight-seeing. We spent about two hours in Westminster Abbey. It is really wonderful. I do wish you could see it before it gets wrecked. Two people in it surprised me—Neville Chamberlain and Charles Darwin. Well, anyway there was a service in one part and the choir boys wear red and white gowns just like the candles you brought [our nephew] Georgie. We walked around that part of the city and visited Westminster Cathedral, too. It is very nice, although not historic.

Sunday, July 2nd

Well, this week has been noisy, too. We haven't done much of note. I had a 48 Tuesday and Wednesday. Went to a little town north (the direction you go to sleep) called Bishop's-Stortford. [Doris and I had left our names at the Knights of Columbus, and from there I got an invitation] to visit the matron of the hospital [there] and thoroughly enjoyed it because I was left to myself quite a bit. Boy, did I sleep. Well, I came back Wednesday night. Friday was rather a bad day. We had a lot of alarms—which don't ring in our building unless something is close. We had all day Saturday off. Doris went out of town. I slept till noon Saturday, then Mac and I went to Richmond in the afternoon. That's the place Cardinal Wolsey[11] had his joint. It's on the Thames River—very pretty. It's north of London and of course the ying bombs all go over there. In fact we could hear the coastal gun barrage. We had supper there, then came back and went downtown. It was marvellous the people that weren't out. We just got nicely home when they started the old slingshots going, and the bombs came thick for a few minutes. For the first time I abandoned my dignity and once got on the floor awfully fast. That particular one hit just down the street. Windows on both sides of us were broken, but none here.

[11] Thomas Wolsey (c.1474–1530) was an English clergyman and statesman who dominated domestic and foreign policy during the early part of Henry VIII's reign. However, he was charged with treason when he failed to secure papal dispensation for Henry's divorce from his first wife, Catherine of Aragon.

Finally I went to sleep and slept until 8 o'clock. The sound of people shovelling up glass is very, very grating. In fact, I'm getting a little irked at Hitler.

Different people react differently. Our Wing Commander runs out into our office away from the windows every time the alarm goes—it's maddening trying to take dictation like that. I worked until 6:30 Friday night. When the alarm goes, I go on calmly, as long as my typewriter doesn't jiggle too much.

Although Friday I sure stopped once. We are on the 6th floor and the thing swayed. Incidentally that was rather messy—an M.A.P.[12] building just down the street. I come home at night, have a fit of the jitters about half an hour, then go to bed, and am ready to start another day. . . . [rest of letter missing]

Our boss, Wing Commander Brearly, was very dour, strict, stiff and distant, and crawled under the only desk we had when there was an alert. We had a wooden table.

July 2.

Dear Mom & Dad:

Just another note. Sorry last week's letter was late, but you know what it's like. By the time we get home, get our supper and sit around, it's bed-time. We usually try to get a little sleep before the 12 o'clock ying bomb. We have the 12 o'clock express, the 2 o'clock freight, and the 6 o'clock milk special. That's the nights—the day's allotments are so frequent we don't name them.

Did you get to Davidson for the first? Hope you did, and the weather was nice. How are the crops, etc.? . . .

. . . I woke up at 8 this morning and couldn't go back to sleep. Between fooling around I have managed to get a couple of letters written. I am going to wash and iron this afternoon, and tonight we are going to Hyde Park to hear the soap-box politicians. It was rainy yesterday and looks the same today, but people are glad of it because they haven't had much.

While I was out last night, the American of Wednesday night (not Tuesday) 'phoned long distance to say he was coming in tomorrow night. The weeks sure fly by—being busy at work and seeing things and going out at night.

I do hope Canadian papers are not exaggerating these new bombs too much and worrying you. They're not to be laughed at, at all, but I'm not worried, so why should you be?

Haven't got in touch with Blanche's friends yet, but really will drop them a line today.

---

[12] Ministry of Aircraft Production

There are so many Canadians over here, you feel as if you knew more people than at home, because you have to consider every Canadian a friend. There are also huge numbers of Yanks, and we feel more of a kinship with them than the English, so you see we're not lonely at all.

I've seen some war, which is what I wanted, so feel more content. Now I want to go to France.

Think I will sign off now & write some brief notes to people. I haven't had any more mail—just two letters forwarded from Lachine. Hope to hear soon—the address is "R.C.A.F. Overseas."

So long for now,
Love,
Teddy.

July 7.

Dear Mom:

Thought I had better send a line this way as I hear the mail has been held up. I have written you ordinary mail every week, so hope you have at least got some mail. I have just had two letters from you, both forwarded from Lachine.

I hope Churchill's speech didn't worry you. It really doesn't seem bad here, and no one is very worried. You just have to use common sense.

I have written to quite a few of the people I am supposed to find, but haven't actually contacted them yet. I still have a few to write to.

I am getting along fine for money. I seem to have enough. I didn't use one traveller's cheque for $20. Ask Dad if I send it back if he can cash it again, whether I should sign it, etc. I haven't cashed that draft yet— I haven't gone on leave. I think I could afford to go on leave without it, but I'll keep it for an emergency.

Guess I will get to work now. I won't write an ordinary letter this week since I am going to Cambridge over the weekend. So long now, don't worry.

Love,
Teddy.

July 7.

Dear Fat:

Just thought I'd drop you a line by Air Mail in case you weren't getting my mail. Of course maybe I thought Winnie had worried you.

Business hasn't been disrupted—we go on working. Our district (where we live) has taken a beating, but all we lost was our windows.

I'm not going to write a regular letter this week because I am going to Cambridge tomorrow afternoon. Cycling and sleeping at Cambridge—jolly, what?

An American friend was in town on Monday. We went to see "Cover Girl." Wait till I tell you about the American Bar here. A bit of 52nd Street on

Piccadilly. Smoke, crowd, Wurlitzer and 4 deep at the bar—American slang and talk. Didn't do much the rest of the week. Have had a couple of good nights' sleep.

I got your book, but am reading it.

Don't worry about me, I'm having lots of fun and dodging the doodle-bugs alright. So far I have bit the dust once (meaning I plopped on my tummy).

I have a great yen to see some American magazines. Could you send me some? Life, Liberty, Redbook, etc. Three or four would please me greatly.

Guess I'll sign off now.

Love

Edna.

W304478
Johnson E. M.
R.C.A.F. Overseas

Stepping out of the tube station on to Kensington High Street, we saw a lot of damage that had been done that day, but it wasn't as bad as we neared Holland Road. However, as Doris was fishing for her door key, I suddenly said, "Never mind." Our front door had been blown outwards. In our room, the glass windows were blown inwards, with shattered glass all over the place. I had an appointment downtown and had to leave right away. "Sorry, friends, do a good job cleaning up." And they did, everybody helping.

July 15.

Dear Mom & Dad:

Well another week. For a change it's been quite quiet. I hope you got the Air Mail I wrote you last week quite quickly. I got three letters from you this week, and two from Blanche, an Air Mail from Dorothy. Have also had mail from the kids at Jarvis. . . .

Monday, 17*th*

Didn't get this finished Saturday. Doris and I started [paper cut by censors]. We got a bus out to his camp, picked up his chum and went to some relation of Gladys' for tea. They were very nice—we sat and gabbed, and then went back to Aldershot, had a cup of tea and got a train. We had a quick trip back, and were in bed by 12. We really enjoyed the day. The boys are coming up to London some week-end soon.

For my birthday I still need bedroom slippers, and I am in fierce need of pyjamas. I can't sleep in my birthday suit as I planned. Can't you see my diving out of our room in an air raid with the bed clothes wrapped around me?

Can you get any jelly powders? If you can, I wish you would send me some. I asked Mrs. Roe what I could get her from Canada. She has everything money can buy here, but did say the family would like some jelly powders.

I have enough money, as we get a living-out allowance. Blanche also was worried as to whether I had enough to travel and see things. I haven't cashed my draft yet.

Well, guess I had better sign off now and either get to work or write a note to Blanche. Of course the very night we didn't get to bed early they started a baby barrage of doodle-bugs which landed out our way. [paper cut by censors] However will go to bed early tonight.

Look after yourselves, and don't work too hard.

Lots of love,

Teddy.

W304478
Johnson E.M.
R.C.A.F. Overseas.

July 17.

Dear Blanche:

Got two letters from you this week—the last written after you got my first one. Now they have started you should get them regularly because I write every week.

July 18

Got another letter from you yesterday. Well, as I started to say, we have been bumming around as usual. Week-end fore last we went to Cambridge Saturday afternoon. The crowd at the station was terrific, but we finally got out. We had a nice night and day. Doris stayed at the Boyles', and I stayed at some friends, the Roes. There were two little girls. They brought me cocoa to bed at night, and breakfast in bed in the morning. Doris and I went out cycling in the afternoon (everybody has a bicycle). Then we had high tea at Boyles' and got a train back. We really enjoyed a good sleep, although I was stiff Monday. We didn't do much through the week. Thursday was Mac's pay day, so we went out to a pub. At 10:30 they closed and kicked us out. A Canadian major who had been sitting next to us laughed and said, "So you've been thrown out of a pub!" We didn't think anything of it, since it wasn't the first one. Anyway, he took us to his apartment right close (we thought it was O.K. since Mac was there. A friend of his who apparently shared the apartment came in in civvies and was introduced as "Major-something." It was a real men's apartment, believe me. The housekeeping was awful. They insisted on making us pancakes, so one them (the first one) tucks a tea towel around his middle, and cooks pancakes. I must say they were good. Then we had coffee in the front room. We thought it was quite an experience meeting a major who could cook. The next morning who should Mac run into but our friend of the civvies, who turns out to be a real live <u>colonel</u>. We had a good laugh over that.

Sunday, Doris and I were determined to go to Aldershot to see Carl, since he 'phoned me twice last week. We got on a train for 11:30. We heard a bomb while we were sitting there, but we pulled out at 11:30—outside the station, sat for awhile, then backed in again. After waiting an hour we finally left by a roundabout way, since the bomb had fallen [censored] a couple of miles away. When we arrived poor Carl had been waiting for us. We went out to his camp by bus. It is nice country, and soldiers abound everywhere you look. We picked up Carl's chum and went up the road to some distant relation of Gladys' for tea. We visited, then went back to Aldershot, looked around there, and got a train back at 9 o'clock. Everything was O.K. by then, so we made good time back. We were dead tired, and managed to sleep until about 5 o'clock. This morning fireworks around our place started at 3, but we were too sleepy to pay much attention.

I have had an answer from Bjarne—he is in France. I had a note from Sheila Church. She is on night shift but will call me up when she goes on days. In case you haven't heard, the Makings have moved to Hereford as Mr. Makings had another break-down. According to her they are in a country cottage doing gardening. I can't get there on a 48, but might go for a day when I get leave. She asked me very nicely to come, anyway.

Doris and I have promised to bat each other's ears down if we get caught with an accent. However, if one does creep up, I regret that I suspicion it will be Cambridge. We are going up there this week-end—we have a whole 48. Since we still can't get leave I have lots of money. I want to see France at the government's expense anyway.

Why don't you give your new boss a chance? You might be able to make something of him.

I was going to suggest you come here for leave—you should be able to hop a bomber—but you wouldn't want to come to England without seeing London, and London isn't particularly restful on the nerves these days. However, the rest of the country is nice.

Carl and his chum are going to try to come up week-end after this.

I keep intending to send you some papers, but forget to do them up. However, I soon will.

How would you like to try and get something for me to give Mrs. Roe? They have everything money can buy. A pair of silk stockings, or a great luxury here is bath salts. Maybe you could get stockings for Mrs. Roe and packages of bath salts for each of the girls. See if you can get Yardley's. Tell mom what you spend—I hope she is keeping our accounts straight. We are getting along fine house-keeping. We can shop off ration cards like a whiz now—and not just a few things are rationed. We can't buy clothes at all. We can get underwear through stores by repayment.

Well, guess I had better close, now, and get to work. See what you can do about my shopping. If you ever see any jelly powder, send them along, too.

Don't work too hard—
Love
Edna.

When I enlisted in 1942, I made 90¢ a day. And by the time I was made Leading Airwoman, I got a big raise—to $1.20 or $1.25 a day. However, when overseas, we were paid in pounds, at Canadian rates, so we were rich. Plus, as there was no barracks for us to live in, we were given a living allowance to cover the cost of our room and meals. I assigned a little bit of my wages to my mother, as was the practice, to pay for things I wanted her to send me.

July 24.

Dear Mom & Dad:
   . . . I had an Air Mail from Marg this week, so at least I know she and Ken are alive.
   I do wonder what Blanche is going to be doing.
   I have pretty well had a letter a week from you. I hope you are getting my mail. In case you didn't get my last letter, I still need pyjamas and slippers for my birthday. We can always use tinned stuff in our business; cookies, etc. I can stand some brown (dusk) lisle stockings. I hope you are keeping my account straight. I started a bank account here—I might get a small accumulation for a leave, although I still have the draft.
   How is the garden? Did your chicks grow alright? Did the Knutsons know Bjarne was in France? It doesn't sound exactly like a picnic.
   English people are the most avid news followers—they would certainly put Canadians' news ignorance to shame. They are always reading either a book or paper on the tube, waiting for a tube or bus, or in any cue [*sic*]—where if you do anything you spend half your time. London isn't quite so bad now, because there aren't so many people here. By this time we have caught on that we are the ones who have the accent and try to use English terms to make ourselves understood a little better. If you have a parcel with some empty space you could send my green slacks, although Doris said she wouldn't bother, because we would soon be home. Things look good, but you know us clerks will be the last ones back.
   Well, guess I'll sign off and scribble a few lines to Blanche. Don't work too hard, and don't worry. Take care of yourselves.
   Love,
   Teddy.

Carl Germain was my cousin, and he was married to Gladys. Bjarne and Elmer Knutson were just boys—not even twenty or twenty-one—from Elbow. They lived two miles down the road from Dad's farm, and the two of them worked for Dad.

The farm was about 3,000 acres—six sections. It was a wheat farm—no animals—although we did have a cow. I lived mostly in Regina, with my mother. Dad went out to Elbow for all of the growing season. My dad always had men who were good with machines to help him work the farm. My dad also had three gas trucks in Moose Jaw. There was a refinery in Moose Jaw, and he had the contract to deliver gas to three towns. The Elbow farm is now one end of the Diefenbaker Dam on Lake Diefenbaker. Dad stayed on the farm until the boys, Bjarne and Elmer, got back. He'd promised them they could rent the place. He and my mother then retired to the West Coast.

My father, James Edgar "Ed" Johnson, became a fairly affluent man, coming from modest beginnings. His first farm was a homestead, outside of Moose Jaw, that potash was later mined on. He also kept Curtiss Jenny airplanes—the Western Airplane Company. But even though that was before I was born, we used to go to airfields on Sunday afternoons to watch planes fly. That's how my love affair with the air force began, although I had no illusions when war broke out that I'd ever be allowed to fly a plane. The Western Airplane Company Hangar is now a History of Transportation exhibit at the Western Development Museum in Moose Jaw and shares space with the world-famous Snowbirds.

My mother was the former Eva Tanner.

July 25.

Dear Blanche:

Another week—not too bad. As far as weather is concerned, I haven't been very hot yet. As far as buzz bombs are concerned, we had more than the previous two weeks, and as far as work is concerned I have been busy. We haven't done much in the way of entertainment. We had a 48 and went to Cambridge Friday night. We had two lovely nights of sleep. We looked around Cambridge stores—I bought a book, "Introduction to Industrial Psychology," and surprisedly found the English have been experimenting for years—but then that is what we find with a lot of ideas new to us.

We were in King's College Chapel—a lovely building, although some of the windows have been taken out. As you remember, Henry VI built it when he founded King's College, the start of the University. We went in some other churches and looked at the college.

Sunday we cycled out to Granchester and had tea in an orchard, *à la* Rupert Brooke. Then we came back to town in a circle. The country is lovely. They boat up and down the little river.

I am wondering if you are working for the objectionable man somewhere else, or if you quit and went home. I suppose you have taken your holidays by now. No leave yet for us—thank heavens for a 48 once a month and Sundays off.

Carl and his chum might come up to London this week-end, but don't know for sure yet if they can get away.

Doris and Mac and I are seeing "Arsenic & Old Lace" tonight. It had better be good for 10 bob a seat. The theatres here start at 6:30—it's rather nice getting home, but rather a rush from work. However, it's on the Strand, not far from us. If Carl comes to town he wants to go to the Windmill, a vaudeville theatre.

Haven't made any new acquaintances this week to tell you about, and there really isn't much to say. The war looks so good; we hope we can get the men sent back home so we can get there by Christmas, but I can just picture A.F.H.Q. being the last unit to break up. However, I haven't seen everything yet.

Doris and I have been talking about joining the Church of England over here. I wonder if they'd take us. Here, like the States, there is no United Church, but I always thought I'd be an Anglican anyway.

I got an Air Mail from Marg this week.

Well, guess I'll sign off. I think I must be getting all your mail alright. Hope you get mine.

So long for now,
Love
Edna.

Historical Note: Rupert Brooke (1887–1915) was a promising English poet who died young during World War I. His poem, "The Old Vicarage, Grantchester," made the church in this charming village of the same name quite famous.

> . . . would I were
> In Grantchester, in Grantchester!—
> Some, it may be, can get in touch
> With Nature there, or Earth, or such.
> And clever modern men have seen
> A Faun a-peeping through the green,
> And felt the Classics were not dead,
> To glimpse a Naiad's reedy head,
> Or hear the Goat-foot piping low: . . .
> But these are things I do not know.
>
> . . .
> Say, is there Beauty yet to find?
> And Certainty? and Quiet kind?
> Deep meadows yet, for to forget
> The lies, and truths, and pain? . . . oh! yet
> Stands the Church clock at ten to three?
> And is there honey still for tea?

July 30.

Dear Mom & Dad:

First, I have to bawl you out for writing an Air Mail and not writing on the side flaps.

Next, I want to be sure you're not worrying. We don't believe anything is happening until we read it in the paper. Anyway, when a bomb comes over it has to get to London, then if it gets here it has to find Kensington High Street, then it has to find 55 Holland Road, then it has to find our room, then if it succeeds in finding that, we will probably be away downtown at work.

Doris' address is   "W302511 L.A.W. Johnson, D.M.
R.C.A.F. Overseas."

I haven't got the parcel yet, but probably will soon, as they have been coming through fairly good (a month to 6 weeks). Carl and Al (his chum) came up yesterday and have just left. We went to a theatre last night and sightseeing today. Saw St. Paul's and Hyde Park—that is, the new things we hadn't seen before. We showed them the palace, Wellington Barracks, Houses of Parl't and Westminster Abbey. . . .

Doris and I have been thinking about joining the English Church—maybe even getting confirmed. What do you think about it? I don't know whether the Church of England is like your Ontario Anglican Church or not.

I suppose Dad is thinking about Harvest. Hope the crop is good so you can have a nice holiday this winter. No leave yet, but I don't really mind it—having Sat. afternoons and Sundays off.

Haven't done anything very exciting this week. We just have to fight to travel—the crowds on trains are terrific—especially weekends.

This week we are going to see Noel Coward's "Blithe Spirit." I just got a letter from Al McLeod saying he was coming to town this week, so there are a couple of nights.

Look after yourselves and don't work too hard. If you ever see any film—any size—send it—I can borrow a camera. If you have any new snaps I'd like to see them.

Love, Teddy.

Aug. 1.

Dear Blanche:

A very ordinary week indeed.

I got a letter from you on Thursday. I don't remember the date, but it was quite good. I got a letter and an Air Mail from mom, and some letters from kids at the station. Mom said she wished I wouldn't go to pubs, but I will certainly tell her that if you can go to night clubs in New York I certainly can go to innocent little pubs in London. Besides I am far more capable of taking care of myself than you are. And another thing, what do you mean—you hope my nerves hold out? You're the one with bad nerves, not me.

I can't figure out what's wrong with your boss. What is? Now if there was something concrete, like our Winco—he's effeminate and fussy and dictates too fast.

We thoroughly enjoyed "Arsenic and Old Lace." It was at the Strand Theatre. Of course, it's an American play and it did sound funny for people with English accents to be referring to Brooklyn and Flatbush, but they were good actors. A lot of theatres with good plays have closed down, so maybe we can catch up with the ones that are running.

We didn't do much the rest of the week. Saturday afternoon Carl and his chum came to town. We made them supper, then went to the Windmill Theatre. You must have heard of it—it's a famous burlesque and vaudeville theatre. I guess the boys saw enough exposed woman [*sic*] to last them a while. Sunday we dragged them out to show them the sights—House of Parl't, Westminster Abbey, the palace, Wellington barracks, St. Paul's, Fleet Street and Hyde Park. Saturday night we got lost (of course) and so I saw for the first time Regent, Bond Street, and Berkeley Square. We cooked a big meal when we got back, and they left at 9 to catch their train. Carl is going on a guard's course with the English Army and then quite likely home. The boys went back satisfied—they heard lots of doodle-bugs, they saw where some had freshly been, and they saw one.

Tonight we are going to Noel Coward's "Blithe Spirit." Next week-end is the infallible English bank holiday. Although we are getting Monday off, we are not even going to attempt to travel. Ordinary week-ends are bad enough. I'm sure Washington even isn't as bad, because there aren't as many people in Washington, and they're not all trying to get out of town.

No, I certainly didn't tell mom about the bombs, although in her letter she said she guessed by the sound of the news I was seeing action enough even for me. Which of course is ridiculous—I'd give a finger to go to France. . . .

I mailed you a few newspapers last week. Don't know if you'll get them or not, but thought you would like to see them. Every time I see something famous, or do something interesting, I think how much you'd enjoy it. Well, I can make you up a list for your trip.

If you ever see anything that resembles a camera or film, buy it and send it to me—that is, anything short of $20. If you can get film, I can always borrow a camera somewhere.

I can't get to Albert Hall like I intended to—they closed it, so now you have to listen to the symphony orchestra over the radio (excuse me, wireless).

Well, can't think of anything else at the moment. Hope you are getting my letters. How about telling me if I'll be home for Christmas or not?.

Love,
Edna.

After a decade of teaching school in various communities in southern Saskatchewan, my sister Blanche accepted a recruiter's call and, in 1943, moved to Washington, D.C., where she served as the personal assistant to the Director of Radio and Radar Supplies for the British Air Commission, a part of the Royal Air Force. The work was top secret—even the carbon paper was shredded, stapled in an envelope and handed to a guard to dispose of, and everything that was typed was kept face down on the desk. She shared an office with the director, so that when he went out of town, she knew exactly what was happening and everything could continue. Blanche remembers it is an exhausting time, but exciting. They worked long hours, especially when a big push was happening overseas, and a lot of interesting people came in the office and were on their telephone list.

Aug. 5.

Dear Mom & Dad:

Another week, practically, and nothing much doing. Have been working pretty hard. I didn't get any letters this week, but got the parcel on the 2nd, which is pretty good for a parcel. Thanks for everything. It was in good condition, except the cookies, which were broken. They carry better in a can—just a plain tin can washed out. We can struggle along on our tea, although it isn't as nice. Hope you didn't run your ration short. I got a box of Laura Secord chocolate today, too. The card said from Blanche, although it wasn't her writing . . . The next parcel you send will you put in some <u>Players'</u> cigarettes. Of course it isn't a habit—I have more will-power than that.

Tuesday night we went to Noel Coward's "Blithe Spirit." It was a riot—we really enjoyed it. We went right from work—everything starts so early here. Tuesday afternoon the information desk phoned to say there was someone downstairs to see me. I couldn't figure out who it could be, but I went down. I looked around stupidly not seeing anyone I knew, then this cute little officer comes up and says, "Edna? I'm Jack Woods." I never expected to see him because Marg never gave me his number, and Jack didn't have my number, and he only knew one initial, but after looking in only a couple of buildings found me. Imagine me being that well known in London! Well, he wanted me to go out Tuesday but, of course, I was going to the theatre with Mac, so we agreed on Wednesday. He met me after work; we had supper at a nice restaurant I know on the Strand, then we went to the new Bing Crosby show "Going My Way," which was on down in Piccadilly. Then we went to the club where he is living, which is not far from where we live, and had tea and sandwiches. Then he brought me home, we talked for a while then he started to walk home, but haven't heard whether he got there or not—it's quite a way to walk.

Last night we came home from work dead tired and didn't do anything but sing a bit and go to bed. Tonight just about the same, except we are both writing letters. We have a nice week-end. I have to work tomorrow afternoon & have Sunday & Monday (English bank holiday) off. Doris has tomorrow afternoon off but has to work Monday. Bill (her husband) finishes his course next week and is going Overseas and is getting indefinite leave, so Doris is getting a week's leave. Incidentally, Jack Woods came down from the same station Bill is at, and he is also on his way Overseas (that doesn't mean Canada), and on indefinite leave.

There are a lot of pigeons around here, and at night they sound just like the owls in the yard up there.

Carl is just a sergeant—don't believe Aunt Ellie's line of bull. He is going on a guard's course with the English army and may go home after it. He really pines for home and Gladys—I don't think he has a great deal of fun, but I know he enjoyed last week-end. He tells me young Dot is thinking about getting married.

Haven't heard from Elmer yet, but mail service in England is very slow. It's no wonder, the crowds that travel on the trains.

My friend Al McLeod (the American) was supposed to be coming to town this week, but haven't seen him yet. London should be pretty nice this week-end—at least there shouldn't be any crowds. The stores will all be closed, though. Well, must sign off now. I owe so many letters it isn't funny. A lot of kids from Jarvis have written to me—even Pat Pound, the civilian girl in the Equipment Orderly Room, wrote to say she misses my efficient hand (hem!). The efficient hand is not getting much practice now.

Well, take care of yourselves,
Love
Teddy.

Jack Woods, who was in the air force, was my sister-in-law Marg's brother. He had just come back from West Africa and was waiting for re-posting.

Aug. 5

Dear Blanche:

Hope you are getting my letters since I have been writing faithfully every week. I think I have been getting all yours, although I didn't get any mail this week—it usually comes in a bunch. . . .

As far as bombs, the week hasn't been too bad. Day before yesterday was hazy and quite a few slipped through. Everyone is waiting for the V-2 with interest, but I think it's propaganda. . . .

. . . Thursday it was warm, and Doris and I were both worn out, so didn't do much—same last night. Both our appetites are off, but expect they will recover—mine always does. Tonight we think we are going to a dance. I have to work this afternoon. Guess I had better sign off & get to work.

Behave yourself—
Love
Edna.

Aug. 12/44.

Dear Mom & Dad:

Haven't done much this week. This is a peaceful Saturday afternoon and I am lying out on the grass in the sun (yes, sun, although it's English) in my shorts. I have just finished writing to Bjarne—I must say it was high time. We did our shopping this afternoon and looked at the shows, but there was a line-up for all of them, so came home. A friend of Doris' and her friend are staying at this house so we all eat together now. It should work out fine. We have a notion to look for a flat, but haven't actually started looking. I got your letter of August 1st this morning.

We didn't go away last week-end, although Doris has gone up to Cambridge for this week-end. I didn't go. . . .

Damed [*sic*] if I can think of anything to say. Too bad you lost out part of a letter—I try to think whether what I write will be censored. . . .

The news over here is all good. Maybe you can set a place for me at Christmas dinner.

I'd kind of like to stay over here afterwards, but they send us home to discharge us. If I took my discharge here and looked around I'd have to pay my own way home. Oh well, I suppose I'm lucky to see the British Isles! Travel to Ireland (Northern) has been reinstated for civilians so I might possibly get there.

I got a letter from Reimer the other day. He is not far away, so I must try and see him. (Excuse the spot of water.)

I really have to quit as I can't think of anything else to say.

Love,
Teddy.

Reimer was a friend from Regina. He was a teacher who boarded at my mother's house there. However, he became so crippled up with rheumatism that he couldn't teach. So, he came down to Ontario to visit Dr. Locke, a famous foot doctor in Winchester. Anyway, Dr. Locke must have done some good, because there he was, in the army. But he worked in a hospital and wasn't doing any hard stuff.

Aug. 13/44.

Dear Blanche:

I got another letter from you this week. They are coming through fine—I think I get them all. I wrote a note to Mr. Brunker yesterday and told them he could read the magazines first if he wanted. We are not supposed to disclose our address, but here is mine—address it "Miss—etc.,

55 Holland Road
Kensington High Street
London, W.14

You had better still send my letters to RCAF Overseas, though.

For my birthday I would like some bubble bath—it's light enough to send—and some clothes. Underwear, pyjamas, <u>stockings</u>, hankies. I hope I don't get too big a supply since I'll be over here another year. . . .

Guess I had better not tell you where I am working, but surely some of your men who go back and forth know. It is a comfort to be working with all Canadians.

Last Monday Mac and I went to the wax works. Very interesting. They really are awfully good. Who should be there in all his glory but McKenzie [*sic*] King. Incidentally, the army boys say that his day is done.

Oh yes, I had a letter from Reimer. He is not far from London, so must try and see him. I just got a letter from Mom. She says one of my letters had been censored and a bit cut out.

No, I haven't seen any of your friends. I have stayed in town the last two week-ends and, boy, we've really slept.

Believe it or not, it hasn't rained since Monday, and more than that, the sun has shone three days in a row.

I hear from a lot of kids at the station, and try to write somebody there fairly often. Jack Mayberry said in a letter that a letter of mine had become quite dog-eared.

As for accent—banish it from your mind. I have just got used to what it must be like trying to speak in a foreign country. People look at us as if <u>we</u> had the accent—not them. We have met some grand people, but if you ask us, we still don't like Englishmen generally. Guess I'll sign off—hope I have told you all I wanted to. So long,

Love
Edna.

Aug. 21

Dear Blanche:

Well, I was out to see Reimer but, anyway, I'll take that when I come to it.

Jack Woods is still in town. He came up to the house again Tuesday and the gang of us Canadians just fooled around and talked. He phoned up Saturday afternoon so I asked him out for supper. We sat and talked, then did the dishes, then Mac and Jack and the two other girls and I went out to a pub. After spending some time there we went to a dance. Thence, after waiting with the boys (we picked up a sailor some place through the evening) for their bus, came home. Sunday Jack and I both went to see Reimer. The station he is on is quite nice. (We walked 2 miles to get to it from the train.) We sat in the sergeants' mess and gabbed, and Reimer got me beer without blinking an eyelash. The staff is all Canadian, and quite a few Saskatchewan boys. Some of them Reimer worked with in Regina. I had quite a visit with a Rogers boy from Riceton. Jack enjoyed himself too. We got back home shortly after 10, had tea and quite a visit with May's boyfriend, then they finally went home.

Doris' husband arrived on leave, and Doris has a week's leave. When they come back they have a room downtown, since Bill has six weeks' leave, so I am by myself. May & Kay have a room upstairs, but we eat together. Oh yes, about Doris—she is from Toronto, she is 24, married a year and a month ago to Bill Johnson, a New Zealander, who is now in England but on embarkation leave, same as Jack. She has a brother who came over here in '39, saw him for about an hour a month ago on his way to France. She has two sisters and a brother at home. Her mother & dad both migrated to Canada from England (wise people).

Friday night Mac and I went to see "Up in Mabel's Room" and really enjoyed it. The rest of the week, other than specified, I stayed home. Tonight I am sure going to bed—after I wash a shirt since I forgot to take my laundry in last week.

I may be moving, but I'll still be in England—much as I would like to go to the Riviera for the winter. English country in winter—brr-rr! If I move maybe some of your men who go back and forth will know about it—doubtless they will.

I got the box on the 18th. Thanks a lot. It was tightly packed and I think everything was in it. That's pretty good time—less than a month. I haven't received any magazines yet, though I am going to Cambridge this week-end I think.

So long now—behave yourself.

You are crazy to work so hard and stand the heat. Why do you stay? You should take a holiday for a few months, especially when your nerves are so bad. Must sign off.

Love
Edna.

Aug. 28

Dear Mom & Dad:

I got your parcel Friday. Thanks a lot. It was in good condition and, as you see, made good time.

I haven't had any mail from you for about a week and a half, so hope you aren't working too hard at the harvest. I have had mail from Blanche in the last week. . . .

Bing Crosby went walking in Hyde Park yesterday and nobody recognized him.

Leaves have started—I get mine early in October and still hope to go to Scotland. Hope the weather isn't too raw. I want to go up to Aberdeen (on the East coast) and see the country around there. Then for the rest of this year's leave, probably in March, I'll see some of the cities of England.

Have you heard about the additional money we're supposed to get on discharge?—50¢ a day—I'll be able to get myself to college yet.

I haven't seen Jack Woods this week, but I think he is still around.

I'll try to get you something real Scotch from Scotland—any suggestions? Must quit now, look after yourselves.

—Love
Teddy.

Aug. 29

Dear Blanche:

Another week—what do you know? I had a letter from you last week, but none from Mom. Didn't do much last week. Had a 48, so went to Cambridge Saturday morning. Arrived Saturday afternoon, didn't do much Saturday—just talked. Sunday morning we went punting on the river and I was stiff yesterday from paddling. It was a hot week-end. Sunday afternoon the girls and I went to the neighbors for tea. The daughter was home from London for the week-end, and they also had a Canadian friend of their son's there. Got the 7 o'clock train back, and was home by 9:30.

Doris' husband is in town on leave, so she is living downtown with him. The other two girls are cooking their suppers, but I decided to eat mine out. I went to the Legion last night for supper, and a boy from the Army Show asked me to go to a show, so I did. I took him home afterwards, collected the gang and we all had tea. Had a typical crazy Canadian time.

Thursday noon Artie Shaw played in the park by our place. Now Lincoln's Inn Fields is supposed to be quiet—it is a collection of law buildings, lawyers' offices, etc. The oldest building was finished in 1492. Well, anyway, just introduce Artie Shaw's music and the effect is wonderful. I don't think English people saw the irony though. There goes the imminent danger signal, so everybody sits and listens.

I got a parcel from both Mom & Blanche last week. Our wingco arrived back yesterday, heaven bless him. Well, haven't heard the doodle-bug yet so it must have gone over some other A.M. building. Had a letter from Barney last week—he's getting lots of excitement. We're going to go out in Elbow some time and give the town lots to talk about.

Must sign off. Will stay home this weekend and write a real letter, although there is nothing to say.

Love,
Edna.

Historical Note: Artie Shaw (1910–2004) was a leading jazz clarinetist and big band leader of the mid-twentieth century. He also dabbled in symphonic music and avant-garde jazz combos and led a U.S. Navy big band during World War II. A famous ladies' man in his day, Shaw was married eight times, including marriages to Hollywood beauties Lana Turner and Ava Gardner.

August 31

Dear Mom & Dad:

Hope you have been getting mail alright. I got a letter yesterday, but that is the only one for about a week and a half, but I just supposed that you were busy harvesting. Also got a letter from Blanche yesterday saying she was leaving for home, but I suppose if she is there now, she will be gone when this arrives. Also got an Air Mail from Marg, but it took about 12 days to come, which isn't so good for Air Mail. She thought Blanche might go out there to see them—did she?

Did I tell you I had another letter from Barney? He has been where it was rather thick, and says he has got so practised diving for a slit trench that he feels just like a gopher. However, I think the gophers I am shooting have a better chance.

Doris' Bill got called back unexpectedly back to his station yesterday, so Doris is back home now, and we are going to take up cooking again—I had been eating out. It is really best, if we have the ambition, because we can have what we want cooked right—not English.

We have had quite a few alerts the last few days, but haven't heard a bomb fall very near for quite a while—guess they're afraid to rouse the ire of the Canadians.

Oh yes, before I forget—will you send $3.60 to the Doubleday Book Club, Toronto. Lo and behold last week what should I get in the mail but a copy of "For Whom the Bell Tolls," and a bill for $3.60. I think I only owe $2.40, but send the billed amount, and I will write them a letter. Apparently they sent a book I didn't get. I will also be getting the August one, because I don't have time after the notice to tell them I don't want it, so I will tell them not to send any more.

I'm afraid I'll have to write the University and tell them not to expect any more theses, because I haven't opened my Philosophy book since I arrived, except to press a rose from Cambridge and a fern from Haselmere in it.

A funny thing happened last night. I stayed downtown to go to Glee Club practice. About 8 o'clock I was outside the High Street Kensington tube station waiting for a bus, when an airman came along and asked me if I worked at Records. I said no, and he said he just thought I might know the girl he was looking for, who worked at Records and lived near there—she had moved and he didn't know where to find her. I said that's too bad, not very sympathetically. He seemed to want the conversation going, and asked me where I was from. I said Saskatchewan, and he said he was too. I asked him what part and he said Elbow, so I asked him his name and he said MacLean. I said pleased to meet you, my name's Johnson from Elbow—he exclaimed, "Not Ed Johnson's daughter!" Baldy MacLean was the last person in the world I was thinking of meeting here, and he didn't even know I was in the Service. I had met him before, but just because of the unexpectedness of it neither of us recognized each other. I think he has gained about 20 pounds. I have lost a little weight, goody, goody, but I'm no sylph yet.

I suppose harvest is well on its way? Are you still going to the Coast as soon as it is done? Let me know right quick when you change address, because I have to have it changed on my documents.

This week-end we are going to stay home and write letters and do our laundry. I think I will leave this to finish then, because I can tell you what we do over the week-end, and I can't think of anything else now.

Sunday Night
Last night May & Kay and I went to a dance. Had quite a nice time. Dances quit at 11, we walked home and got here at 11:30. Then we had tea, but I thought it was too nice to stay in and go to bed so I went up to see if Mac was in bed. He wasn't so we went out for a walk. Got back about 12:30. Got up this morning about 11, had breakfast, then Doris and Bill (did I mention that he came back to finish his leave and they got a room in the house?) Mac and I and the housekeeper's young son went to the Tower of London. We just got there in time to catch a tour. It is very interesting, but too much to write about. The men at the gates and ones who take around the tours are real Yeomen of the Guard, Tower Wardens. You should see their outfits—just like pictures, really.

I haven't heard from Jack Woods for a while, so don't know where he is.

We have had supper, finished the dishes and are just sitting around—Bill reading and Doris and I writing letters. Think I must sign off, and see if I can catch up on some back ones. I keep getting letters from people in Canada—didn't know I had so many friends, and suppose I must answer them all, because I like getting letters.

So long now, take care of yourselves—
Love,
Teddy.

Baldy McLean was a guy from Elbow. I never cared very much for him and, in fact, I don't know if I had seen him very much in Elbow. But in London we saw quite a bit of each other. He was from home.

Sept. 3rd

Dear Blanche:
Hope you have had a nice leave and are feeling better for it. Also hope Washington has cooled off a bit.

This week I got a Life, and a Colliers and Liberty which were addressed to R.C.A.F. Overseas. I also got a nice note from Mr. Brunker saying he hadn't got the magazines yet, but would certainly send them to me when they arrived. No doubt they are held up because his section have moved from Clarendon Place to Thames House—better get your address book up to date. No doubt they have moved into the office emptied by the section that evacuated (according to the latest and best-prepared propaganda). One of the sergeants says last week—"Well, pack your bags, girls, this Headquarters is moving to India!" I guess I can tell you now—three weeks ago we were told to pack our bags and, no fooling, and be ready to evacuate on short notice. However, that has blown over, so I guess we can remain here leading the life of Riley. What was your W/C doing to get pale and weary looking?

My phone number at home is Western 4556—which place I frequent between 7 o'clock at night and 8 o'clock in the morning (the nights I am home). . . .

I'm sorry I kept forgetting to tell you. I started out to Lachine with quite a few stamps and my pearls that I was going to give you. When I sent my suitcase home I sent them in it. If Mom hasn't sent them to you, or found them, she could send you the stamps anyway.

Wednesday night I ran into Baldy MacLean from Elbow quite by accident. In fact, it was almost a pick-up, and when we found out who each other was we had a real good laugh about it.

Last night May and Kay and I went to a dance. I've always told the absolute truth to people who asked intelligent questions about Canada but, so help me, last night I strung my first line. Two objectionable Englishmen from the West End had such fantastic ideas that I couldn't help it. I told them I went out with my Dad shooting cattle rustlers. Afterwards a Canadian Flight Lieut. pilot saw us killing ourselves laughing and wanted to know why. He said, "You shouldn't tell these people things—they don't know from nothing!" Then proceeded to tell us how many wars he had started by himself. More I see of Englishmen the less I think of them. Do you remember Margaret Halsey's "With Malice Towards Some"?[13] Well, my book is going to be a scorcher beside hers.

Well, I must go to bed. Take it easy, and be good.
Cheerio—
Love
Edna.

Sept. 10

Dear Mom & Dad:
Got your letter dated Aug. 22 last Monday.

---

[13] Margaret Halsey (1910–97), a U.S. novelist best remembered for her witty novels that lampooned the English and their customs. A bestseller, *With Malice Towards Some* was published in 1938.

Glad Blanche got home after all. She probably needed the rest. Is she any more gray? I pulled out a gray hair last week—not faded blonde, real gray. I hope you haven't lost too much crop—it would be terrible if you had to stay on the farm for the winter.

I have had two parcels from you—I think I mentioned them both. The cookies in the second one were fine, but too near the soap. However, that's nothing—we had cocoa made out of chocolate powder a girl in the office got, and it tasted of Pink Clover dusting powder.

Our Wing Commander arrived back from Canada, and after keeping everybody jumping for two weeks has now gone on leave. The guy that I do all his work got his Flight Lieutenant last week. When he came back from the tailor of course I whistled expressively, looking at his arm.

Really haven't done much all week. Monday night did my laundry. Tuesday night went to Glee Club practice. Wednesday night ate supper downtown, Thursday I ate out, too. Friday night we had to work for a little while.

Yesterday I went for dinner with a girl in our Directorate. We went out to a supposedly black market place and had fried eggs. Since there is no egg allocation this week I guess it is alright. They gave you a loaf of French bread and you hacked off what you want. Oh yes, we also had about a quarter of a pound of butter. Then we had more warm bread, and loads of jam with it. I can't imagine writing home about an ordinary meal like that if I was still in Canada, but here it's different. In the office our chief topic of conversation is food. We can talk about it for hours.

After we decided to go to the British Museum. Found it closed for the War. They moved the best stuff out at the beginning and the rest of it got destroyed by bombs. Well, that was no go, so we went to the National Art Galleries on Trafalgar Square. They have a big exhibition of war artists' paintings, and a whole room of Canadian paintings. There were several by men in our section—our directorate includes Historical. They were all good, and I could spend more time there. Again, the old and valuable paintings were removed. We had tea, and then went to the Sadler's Wells Opera which was the "Bartered Bride." It was very good. After that—about 9:30—we looked for some place to eat. Most restaurants were full, but we got into a Greek place just off Piccadilly and had steak and onions.

There are so many novelties and oddities here that you can't get at home, that I can't resist the cutest. I buy something every once in a while, and am going to gradually send them to you for Christmas presents. You'll have to do the wrapping. I don't want to send them all at once in case of loss.

You know every once in a while something strikes me funny and I kill myself laughing. You have to have a sense of humour to stand this country—I don't know how the English have survived all these years. Last Sunday when we were going to the Tower, we had to change tube trains. We were standing on the platform with quite a few other people, hopefully waiting. We hear a rumble coming from the dark tunnel, and everybody stands up and walks over the edge, ready to jump on the train. Well, what should come chugging up but one of these miniature locomotives with a whole string of their toy gravel cars behind. Well everybody just looked at it stupidly. It was so darned funny, I still chuckle over it. Did you hear about the guy who hollered "whoa!" at a restaurant door, and 2 people who were eating meat choked to death.

Guess I had better do my shining, take a bath and go to bed, as I never seem to get enough sleep. Have had a lovely lazy Sunday. Did some washing and ironing, played the piano for awhile. Didn't even get dressed all day. It is sunny, but not warm. Just about like a Fall day at home. I wore a shirt on Saturday since our building is chilly.

You might put a bottle of cod liver oil or something in the next parcel. Be sure it's well packed. Maybe some concentrate capsules would pack better, although I don't think they're as good. I'll look and see what I can find here.

Cheerio for now,
Love
Teddy.

Friday, September 15th

Dear Mom & Dad:

Just a note to let you know I got the parcel Wednesday. It had carried well. The pyjamas fit O.K. although not washed yet. Thanks a lot—everything was needed.

I got a parcel from Blanche today with some things she got me for the Roes. It was O.K. except for the fact that it was about 2" deep in powder.

I got your letter dated Sept. 1 on Monday. Pretty good. Got an Air Mail from Blanche yesterday that she mailed from Regina.

I have a chance to take a week's course at Oxford, so am going there for my leave. It's just a general course that runs from Monday to Saturday. I might go to Edinburgh one day before, although it is quite a trip. Ireland is now open, and I swear I'm going to see it, so hope I get another leave while I'm here.

What do you mean the slippers were too small? Hope you didn't try them on Blanche. If they're big enough for you they will be lots big for me.

The news is so good that everybody is happy. I would like to go away this weekend, the weather is so nice, but I have a cold and, anyway, I'm staying on duty this afternoon for the corporal, because she just got married and her husband is in town. Don't know how I got this cold—it's the first I've had since I came (much to my surprise). There seem to be a lot around, although the weather is quite nice.

Glad to hear the crop is good. I miss the farm during harvest.

This morning the Wing Commander and F/L Saunders are on leave, S/L Holman is on temporary duty so we have only one officer. Pauline is on leave, and the corporal got the morning off, so there are only 3 of us girls. I haven't a great deal to do, but am dreading Monday when both officers come back with lots of work and only two stenos.

Well, think I must sign off. Don't worry, and have a nice holiday when harvest is over. Be sure and save lots of dills—they should be about right by Christmas. (You can dish me up a plate of Christmas dinner, but don't wait for me if I'm late.) Am buying a few odd Christmas presents that I will send to you. There is a lot of cute stuff here, if you can afford it.

Cheerio for now—
Love
Teddy.

Sept. 18/44.

Dear Blanche:

Came back early at noon in an endeavor to get this written, since tonight I must put up my hair, and should do a washing, and of course our evenings are very short when we cook our own supper. Got the parcel on Thursday. I'm sure the Roes will be very happy—here is contents—

2 chocolate bars, 2 pkgs. gum, 1 box face powder, 2 boxes dusting powder, 1 pr. silk stockings, 3 boxes Jell-O, 1 bar soap & a box Kleenex. The bottom of the face powder had split, and tops of dusting powder had slid open—so naturally there was powder all over everything.

Haven't done much exciting this week. Caught a terrible cold, so have gone to bed every night since Tuesday (Glee Club night), including Saturday. Was duty clerk Saturday afternoon. Sunday I went to a special commemoration service of the Battle of Britain in Westminster Abbey. I don't know when I've seen so much brass in one spot. The sidewalk and road were full of people watching the notables come out—we went out the back door. You had to have tickets to go, and the place was full. I didn't think the sermon was particularly nice—maybe it was and I couldn't understand it. As for the service, bobbing up and down didn't bother me, but when they <u>chanted</u> the psalms and the Creed that did floor me. It wasn't particularly musical either.

I met a girl for lunch before the service. I was supposed to meet her at the station at 12 o'clock, so got up early and rushed out, then when I got there wondered why all the clocks said 11—I had forgotten to put my watch back—we are only on ordinary summer time now.

Well, after the service we wandered around Piccadilly and Leicester Square noting that most of the shows were already full. At last we found a show with some room and "Once Upon a Time" was playing. We enjoyed it. Then we went to the Hong Kong restaurant and had a real Chinese supper. It wasn't as good as Wah Kai's in Hamilton (no Fan Tan game though). I got home shortly after 10, and went to bed.

Monday night

Had supper, did the dishes, got my hair up and am going to finish this. Worked really hard today, and am tired. . . .

Did I tell you I got your Air Mail from Regina last week? You certainly did your year's shopping. Did I tell you about the comment my glasses cause here? Nearly all English people comment on them, but if you could see English glasses you wouldn't be surprised. One guy, in trying to convey to me the impression that he thought I was a bit hoity-toity (with much repeated West End accent and sign language) said to me (I think), "Now look here, platinum specs . . ."

I'm bound I'm going to Scotland on my leave even if only for a day, which it might—I bet I'll be wishing for my fur coat.

Well, I must go to bed, or I'll lose my beauty sleep. However, the bags under my eyes won't go away short of 3 weeks of sleep. I never saw such a country for tiring you out. Well, cheerio for now. How about contacting family, fairy Godmother, Father Christmas, D.M. & S. or McKenzie [*sic*] King and rooting me out a camera? Hope you straightened out the money I owe you with Mom. Toodle-oo again.

Love
Edna.

P.S. I mailed your "The Sky's the Limit" on Saturday. Hope you get it alright. Let me know when it arrives.

The Glee Club in London wasn't a very long-lasting thing, not like the Glee Club I had belonged to at Jarvis. It was a very lively Glee Club, and we often performed in the surrounding communities.

I wore rimless glasses, which they didn't have in England, at least during the war, so they occasionally caused people to comment. However, because I was posted overseas, I had to get service glasses, because they were the only ones that would fit under a gas mask. They were little round things with silver rims—horrible.

Sept. 24

Dear Blanche:

Got your letter of Sept. 11 this week. Sounds like not a bad trip you had, but you should see the trains here. You <u>can</u> travel for 20 hours without running off the edge, and there are no diners, and you have to be really something to get a berth, and the crowds are terrible.

"Wilson" is playing in the West End now, but it doesn't appeal to me at all.

Yes, I saw your dear boss. He wrote me a letter which took me a week to get although it only travelled a couple of miles. I went to dinner with him Friday night, and was suitably bored. I hope his report in triplicate will be quite satisfactory. As you are well aware, by this time my morals are quite intact, and any of your snoopy friends wouldn't find out if they weren't. He brought me home, so I asked him in. He didn't think much of our room, but it's good enough for anybody else we bring home.

There, there, hold your top, I didn't antagonize him and was sweet as pie, and the girls in the office enjoyed my little encounter.

I received three more parcels of magazines this week. Did you get the letter with my home address? It is

55 Holland Road,
Kensington High St.,
London, W.14.

Everybody usually says, "Kensington?—oh that's the place that got so many doodle-bugs," and that's no lie. Something else has been happening in London but nobody knows just what, and it's sure kept dark.

I am going to Stratford-on-Avon next week-end, but don't know whether you deserved to be told about it or not.

So long for now (or, as the Romans say—"Cheerio")
Edna.

Sept. 24

Dear Mom & Dad:

Another week gone by. It is really like Fall, and today is rainy and windy. I just got up at 1:30, and don't think I'll bother dressing. Doris has gone up to see Bill this weekend, and I am taking it easy.

Wednesday night I started out to find this school where I'm taking philosophy. I went to the tube station that I thought it was nearest, but discovered I had quite a little walk. At least somebody I asked knew where it was, so I didn't have much trouble. When I got there I discovered another tube station just down the street from it. Well, when I had finished walking I was in Lambeth, and what a district! I didn't do the Lambeth walk, I did a very brisk walk straight to the school. When I came out, of course, it was black dark, but I spotted a man with a flashlight and followed him—I made a good guess, he ended at the tube station. The classes should be interesting—the lecturer is a Dr. Lewis from London U. There is really an odd collection of people taking the class—all the way from 60 to 18.

Friday night I went to dinner with Blanche's boss. Can't say I enjoyed it immensely, and I have just written her a very sharp letter over which she'll be mad. Well, it also makes me mad that she thinks I'm not capable of looking after myself and, anyway, if I did go to Hell, she doesn't have to admit that I'm her sister when I see her there.

Anyway it's all superfluous since she and I think the same way anyway, but I don't go around trying to make other people think the way I do.

Last night I went to a dance with May & Kay rather than stay in. We had a nice time. Walked home and were in by a quarter to 12.

I got an air mail letter from Dorothy this week. Also a birthday card from Marg (and Ken, but Kenny hasn't written to me since I came—guess Marg is too handy). I got a letter from Faith Coldridge, a girl in Regina. She wanted me to tell her about New York—imagine! and here I am in the heart of the Empire!

Can't seem to find your last letter. The kids from the station write me all the time, and it is sure amazing how it changes. Both equipment officers that I worked for are gone now.

Next weekend I am going to Stratford-on-Avon, if I can get a place to stay, so won't write you until Monday when I come back.

I have the gas on (you know—gas grate in the fire-place) to get the room good and warm because I want to wash my hair. As usual it has grown fast and is quite long now, and I have to keep putting it up.

I suppose harvest will be over by the time you get this. I don't feel as if I've had any summer at all. No wonder English people are all pale and thin.

I haven't been up to Cambridge lately because of my cold, but hope to get rid of it soon. I haven't finished my halibut capsules yet, but am taking them. Doris bought some tonic and I make her take it. It's funny—I say, "Take your tonic," and she says, "Do I have to?" but I say, "Yes." After a little arguing she takes it—just like a little girl. I'm not used to people doing what I say, but she does, and it rather shakes me.

Really must sign off—I've got so many letters to write—as usual. Guess I'll get something to eat although I'm not hungry, and then wash my hair.

Mrs. McLean brought me breakfast in bed this morning—she's spoiling me, definitely. Don't know who's going to do it after the war. Well, cheerio for now—lots of love and stuff,

Your Teddy.

My night class was a course in Industrial Psychology. I just decided it was something new—probably growing. It was in Lambeth—a grim district. Coming home after dark I had to traverse the people settling down for the night in the tube station. They practically filled the platform. A sad view of London's war.

Historical Note: Lambeth Walk is a street in North Lambeth, between Kensington Cross and the Thames, and for many years was the site of a thriving street market before it was badly damaged by bombing during the Second World War. Lambeth Walk is also a song, a dance, and two films. The original Lambeth Walk was an evening promenade by the predominantly poor residents of North Lambeth. It was popularized in a song and dance of the same name for the 1937 musical comedy *Me and My Girl*.

Any time you're Lambeth way,
Any evening, any day,
You'll find us all
Doin' the Lambeth Walk.

> Every little Lambeth gal,
> With her little Lambeth pal,
> You'll find 'em all
> Doin' the Lambeth Walk.
>
> Everything free and easy,
> Do as you darn well pleasy,
> Why don't you make your way there
> Go there, stay there.
>
> Once you get down Lambeth way
> Ev'ry ev'ning, ev'ry day,
> You'll find yourself
> Doin' the Lambeth Walk.

Oct. 4

Dear Blanche:

Sorry this is late, but will write again over the weekend anyway. Didn't do much over the week, but went to Stratford-on-Avon on the weekend. Went up Friday night, and after groping around the strange town in the dark, the service club got us a place to stay with a very nice lady who <u>loves</u> Canadians. We didn't get up until 10:30 Saturday morning, but got cracking and saw nearly everything there. It's lucky we did, because everything was shut Sunday. We did good business in a curiosity shop. I bought a pair of George III pewter salt cellars, a swell piece of meerschaum carving (which, as I carried from place to place, other collectors looked at enviously), and a Victorian old book of "Humorous" Poetry. Also got some postcards and bookmarks with views. Was going to send you a bookmark, but it is too long for the envelopes I have.

We saw Shakespeare's birthplace. It has quite a few cases with old documents, an old school desk, chest, etc. Three Americans took us in their truck out to Anne Hathaway's, which is out of town. (I forgot to tell you I went up with a girl in our directorate.) The cottage is really sweet, and has quite a lot of furniture, and even dishes. The boys brought us back to town and we didn't see them any more. We had tea in one of Shakespeare's daughter's houses made into a restaurant—Judith Quinney's. Then we went to the house where Bill lived the last part of his life. They have a museum in the house which is very interesting. The gardens are lovely—complete with wishing well. By this time it was raining and we went back to the house and cleaned up. Then we went to the theatre. It is a beautiful building—quite new—1932. They play Shakespeare all summer, and we were just too late, but saw "Acacia Avenue" which was quite good. For a small town they certainly keep a big theatre going. But then I heard somebody say, "Shakespeare is Stratford's industry." We went back to the house and Mrs. Cartwright made us something to eat, since the town burghers rolled up the sidewalk behind us all the way home.

Sunday we finally got out about 12:30. Saw the memorial statue and walked down by the river in the park. Very pretty. We walked around Trinity church but didn't go in since there was Sunday School on, and didn't feel like going.

We got our train back at 6 o'clock. Got a seat to Leamington (about an hour) but had to stand on the Birmingham train. However, there was a gang of us and we had not a bad time.

Had a really nice week-end and am glad I went.

I'm not taking a 48 with my leave since I don't go to Oxford until Monday, so am going to stay home over the week-end and get cleaned up (and rested, since I'll have to get up every morning).

Have been very busy this week doing the summaries, which are to me a lot of nonsense.

Got a letter from you last week. Have been getting them quite regularly.

Must get to work now. So long,

Love

Edna.

I think I found out about the course at Oxford from the Education section. It was a very small section but, boy, a chance to go to Oxford! Well, that was a treat. Plus, they didn't charge us leave for it. That's also why Bert Wilson, my future husband, was there, taking the same course. As it was too soon after the Invasion, he wasn't allowed to take holidays, so he took a course instead.

Oct. 10

Dear Mom & Dad:

I shall attempt to get a note off to you since I didn't over the week-end. I am at Oxford waiting for a lecture to begin.

Last week Baldy & Nicky Gaines came up Tuesday night and I did my laundry. Wednesday night I went to class. Thursday being my birthday the gang from the house went to the pub. Friday night we stayed home (I beg your pardon—we did go out Friday night—to the ballet, and it was wonderful—I could see it every night). Saturday night we had supper on the floor in front of the fire-place, because I got a parcel from Dorothy. Sunday we went with some kids to the Canadian Legion for turkey dinner, but were too late and only got goose, but it was good. We picked up a couple more men and went to see "Dragon Seed" which I didn't think was so good. We then went to the Ontario Club for supper. It has just recently been opened and is very nice.

Well, Monday I came out here. The train was quite full but I got a seat. I managed to find the college (Balliol) and registered and had tea. 68 men were here and me the only female. Well, I doubtfully settled down in my room, then with two Can. boys (thought I'd just better start with two) went out to see the town. We got back just in time for dinner (at 7 o'clock). After that we had some opening remarks by the master (or something). He was a scream. Then the room instantly broke into heated discussion groups. I found myself discoursing the Canadian trade problem.

This morning we had a lecture on the British Gov't, and why it is that way, and a lecture on the history and customs of Oxford. This afternoon we went on a tour of the colleges in small groups. We walked and walked, but all the colleges and churches are lovely.

You should see my "room." It consists of a very large study with bookcase, desk, cupboard, large square table, chairs, large fireplace, window seat and lovely rug on the floor. There is a small bed room off it with bed, cupboard, table & chest of drawers. Really swank. We eat in a large dining hall with old oak tables and benches. We have lectures in a classroom with big school desks.

Because there are only 3 girls they moved some men in the bottom floor of our "stair-case" (group of rooms around one stairs which is a separate part of the building all by itself).

Well, will post this and hope you get it alright. Will tell you about the rest of the week when I write next week-end. Don't know quite all the men yet, but I will—give me time.

So long for now anyway,
Love
Teddy.

Oct. 14th

Dear Blanche:

I don't know how to go about telling you about Oxford in a letter. Guess I will have to tell you the details later. There's something about English life that sucks you in, and it's as if you were wrapped up in cobwebs and couldn't brush them off—it clings. You have to feel it to recognize it, and once you do you understand why England doesn't snap out of it. The Oxford feeling confirmed that and, experiencing it, you fell as if you had sunk further.

Oxford has some big brains, and in hour-long lectures they tried to impart some to us. There were some good brains on the course, too. There was an American Lieutenant Colonel, a Canadian Brigadier-General, and an English Naval Commander, and everything else down. The arguments that went on were fierce and continuous and if a private didn't agree with a major's view he told him so.

Oxford has a population of 100,000, but the Univ. doesn't dominate the town as it used to. There are 26 different colleges—each one a complete unit—i.e. you can take every subject at every college. Our course was at Balliol College. I can't begin to explain the system of hollow buildings with a

Edna at Oxford, October 1944.

"quadrangle" in the centre—several joined up. We lived in the college, and as Mr. Alington expressed it—were considered as honorary under-graduates. Incidentally, my opinion of English humor has improved, since Alington was a perfect scream. Here is a list of the lecturers:—

I.D. Jones on the British State
Rev. R.R. Martin on Oxford
M.R. Ridly on Shakespeare
Rev. J.N.D. Kelly on Political Theory
Dr. H.G. Hanbury on The Law Courts
Dr. C.K. Allen on "What is Democracy?"
Mr. Lionel Curtis on "Decision and Action"

Each lecture was a little over an hour, each followed by good discussions. They were all in the mornings. All the old boys knew what they were talking about. The most outstanding is Mr. Curtis who has written several booklets on post-war governments and primed us for ideas. He has been a brilliant statesman (one of the back-room boys) since the Boer War. He sat in on the conference of Paris and the Versailles Treaty. He is translator, expounder and continuer of Lord Lothian's ideas. I took back-bone short-hand notes to develop into a short article on each lecture. Aside from an awfully good prodding of my mind (which I badly needed) I had a whale of a good time. There were 70 men, 2 A.T.S.[14] girls and me. The majority were Canadians and Americans. The senior officers took it upon themselves to regard me paternally, giving me conversational pats on the head, as it were. The junior officers and ranks took it upon themselves to ensure that I was having a good time and was never without at least 3 men to talk to. In the mornings I concentrated on the lectures, and in afternoons and evenings I concentrated on being Canadian for the boys. I never went out with less than 3 men (don't laugh—after being in London I deserved a week of that). Wednesday night I was quite astounded to discover I had to bid good night individually and sentimentally to no less than five.

I arrived Monday afternoon about 4 o'clock, and after tea went to look at the town with an army and Air Force chap. Monday night there were numerous groups of arguers in the common room, which broke up about 10:30. Tuesday afternoon we were taken on a tour of the colleges and churches in small groups. The group I was with turned out to be a gang which pretty well stuck together the rest of the week. Tuesday night we were given a dance at Rhodes House by Mrs. Allen. There were hostesses for the men, consisting of Dons' wives and diplomats' daughters. Although neither, I had a lovely time. Naturally I couldn't refuse to dance, although my feet were worn to my knees. A gang of us went to the American Red Cross after for coffee & doughnuts.

Wednesday we went to Stratford-on-Avon by bus. I saw the church this time. We went to the theatre and saw the Ballet Joos, arrived back at 6:30. Our gang was going to go to a dance that night but couldn't get in, so went to a quaint pub, the Mitre, very old, and from there to the Red Cross for coffee and doughnuts. Thursday afternoon we went through the Bodleian Library. Some of the old books are very interesting. Thursday night we went to a musicale given by a Miss Deneke and a Dr. Walker, who is a marvellous old man. He is old & bent and short-sighted, but still accompanies beautifully and is still an authority on music. We had the honor of hearing someone who, it appears, is world famous, but whom I have never heard of. However she is a marvellous violinist. I have seen her name but it is pronounced "Yaleenee Darahnyae." The musicale was at Miss Deneke's home in the music room, which held two Steinway Grand pianos, about 36 people, and there was still room for a swing band (Heaven forbid!). Afterwards there were soft drinks and sausage roll bites in the dining room with a lot of "So pleased to meet you" stuff. Oh yes, I was quite civilized and complimented Miss D. prettily. I don't think any grand ball or exclusive drawing room could jar me now.

---

[14] Auxiliary Territorial Services (ladies branch of regular British army).

Friday afternoon & evening we had free, so I went to the show in the afternoon and a dance at night with the boys. Came back to London early this afternoon with the boys, so have tomorrow to recuperate form a week of late nights and continual going. I wouldn't have missed it for anything. The lectures alone were worthwhile.

I found several rolls of magazines from Mr. Brunker when I came back. I must write him and thank him again. He cuts out the stamps very neatly.

Heavens! I have to write all this again to Mom—might as well start copying it.

Oh, by the way, you will be disappointed to hear that although there were only 3 females, every lecturer said, "Good morning, <u>ladies</u> and gentlemen."

I still have a 48 coming this month but don't know where I am going. Probably Cambridge. Must sign off now. Guess since I am an Oxford graduate I can say, "Cheerio."

Love
Edna.

P.S. I spent about 3 shillings. This [letter] sounds pretty good after I read it over—do you mind keeping it for my future reference?

October 14th

Dear Mom & Dad:

Just got back from Oxford this afternoon, and must say I had a wonderful week.

They are some awfully smart men who lectured to us an hour at a time. Of course people on the course weren't so dull either, or they wouldn't have had any desire to go there. . . .

<u>October 17</u>

Still this isn't posted. Found 2 letters and parcel from you when I came back. Everything was swell—the pyjamas fit and the butter was perfectly fresh. Hope it didn't run you short, because we really don't mind margarine. Anyway the butter was a real treat. The shortbread is nice, too, just broken on top.

When I came back I find parades have started again. Everyone in London also has a cold, so I instantly caught one.

Sunday night went to the Nuffield Centre (a service club) to a dance. It was very nice. Last night I doctored and went to bed. Must do the same tonight.

Must quit now so I can get this off today.
Much love,
Teddy.

Surprisingly, baked goods and even butter did not go bad when shipped to people serving overseas. They were usually packed in cans, Roger's maple syrup pint cans being a popular choice.

Oct. 20/44.

Dear Mom & Dad:

Will write this so I can get it away this week-end. I wrote last week-end all about my stay at Oxford, but suppose you will get this [Air Mail] letter first.

Had a letter from Barney. He's in Belgium now, but I suppose you know that.

Haven't done much all week. Went to class Wednesday night. Boy, it seems London gets darker all the time. The tiny lights only make it worse by making reflections in the pavement, which is wet and shiny. Yes, it's rained every day this week, but the grass is green and there are a lot of flowers around—dahlias and zinnias, I think.

The former equipment officer I used to work for is here. I met him in the Ontario Club on Wednesday. We were quite pleased to see each other.

They have started morning parades again—at 8:30, too, which means no dallying around in the morning. We've had an alert every night for nearly two weeks, but I haven't seen or heard a doodle-bug since my birthday. Guess they discovered it was no use looking for me.

I suppose you don't care, but just for your information, Tony is missing. I didn't even see him. Right now, as far as I'm concerned, the Germans could have England and everything in it. It's a feeling everybody gets when they run up against a brick wall—I've seen it in lots of men.

Well, must close this and climb into bed. Doris has gone to York for the weekend to see her brother-in-law. I get a 48 next weekend, and might go to Canterbury. I wish I were home just for tonight, and back again tomorrow.

So long for now,
Lots of love,
Teddy.

Oct. 22

Dear Blanche:

Didn't get any mail at all this week—suppose it is held up somewhere. Last weekend I wrote you all about Oxford, so you should get it shortly after this [Air Mail].

I caught a beauty of a cold when I came back and am still trying to shake it. I have just got up and it is about 3:30. Mrs. McLean brought me tea about 9:30, then breakfast about 11, so I still stayed in bed. I came home yesterday after work, tidied up the room, had supper, did a bit of studying and went to bed. Mac wanted me to go to the show, but I had seen what he wanted to see, so didn't go. This afternoon Baldy McLean phoned & wanted me to go out to dinner, but I decided to stay in. Pretty good of me, eh?

Doris is on a 48 and went to York to see her brother-in-law.

Didn't do anything through the week except go to class Wednesday night. London is blacker than ever it seems to me, and these rainy nights don't help it any.

I sure don't know what to do with my hair—it is so long & taggy I have to put it up every night. I suppose I'll get disgusted, get it cut, and eventually get another permanent for about 3 guineas, which doesn't sound much if you say it fast.

I still hear from Barney—he is in Belgium now, and Elmer is still in France. I checked up on him. Tony is missing on operations. He was with an R.A.F. squadron.

Haven't been very busy at work, since there's only been about one officer in at a time all week. Good thing, since I haven't felt like settling down to work.

Last Wednesday a gang of us went down to the Ontario Club for lunch at noon and I ran into F.L. Page who was S.E.O.[15] at Jarvis—my former boss. He was quite pleased to see me. He has just arrived, and is going to be at H.Q. Too bad I'm not still in equipment.

They have started concerts again in Albert Hall. I never did get to hear Sir Henry Woods (is that his name?) but the London Philharmonic plays Sunday afternoons, and I must get around to going. The trouble is Sunday is always our day of rest—doubly.

There really doesn't seem to be much to write about, so guess I might as well sign off.

It's days like this that make me want to go cut the balloon cables and let the island sink.

So long for now—take care of yourself and don't fade away on that diet.
Love,
Edna.

Oct. 30/44.

Dear Mom & Dad:

Well, how is everything, and are you getting the farm tucked up for the winter?

I didn't do a great deal this week—Tuesday night Doris and I went out with a couple of P.O.'s she knew in Canada. Both finished their tour and are hoping to get back home. We collected Mac and another girl and went to a dance at Hammersmith & tried to see if the bouncer really would bounce anyone.

Wednesday night I went to class, Thursday & Friday nights stayed in. I was on a 48, so got up Saturday morning and went up to the Roes' at Cambridge. They were glad to see me as usual, and I had a nice quiet time doing nothing.

---

[15] Senior Equipment Officer

Poor Baldy! He was supposed to come down Tuesday night, and we waited for him for awhile, but left without him. He arrived later and Mrs. McLean told him I said to 'phone Thursday. He didn't 'phone so he must be mad. Tsk! tsk!

The other day I got a letter with a snap in it of myself signed, "Love, Wilfred." That sure had me stumped. I couldn't think of any Wilfred, but after studying the snap, decided it was taken on a Canadian train, and then placed the guy as an S.P.[16] on the train from Winnipeg to Toronto, and to whom I lost a dollar at Lachine on a bet on my leaving time.

I also received a mystery letter today, and decided it was from an A.T.S. girl. It's amazing the people I hand my address to and then forget.

Haven't got any pictures from the boys of Oxford yet, but am still hoping.

Well, I guess the gang had a rare time Saturday night. Mac & Jim had got 2 chickens (we asked no questions) and after being out pubbing, came in and insisted on picking them in our room. What a mess! Then they gutted them in their own room, waking up the whole house. However, we had the whole house for chicken sandwiches last night. Write you next weekend.

Love
Teddy.

We didn't see much of Jim. Although he had a room in our house, he didn't stay there. But he was very handy in the black market. Jim's father was a Hudson's Bay factor at Tuktoyaktuk, Northwest Territories.

Sunday, Nov. 5

Dear Mom & Dad:

Guess I'll start this tonight, even if I don't finish it. Got a letter from you this week dated Oct. 17. Hope all my letters eventually get to you.

Imagine Keith a father! I can't. Thanks for banking the cheques. Use them if you need them, because they're easy to cash. Did you give Blanche any money for me? Did the girl think you were still crazy when you looked after my coat storage?

Imagine getting harvest over—you'll be able to leave the farm early. Looks as if they'll have to let people shoot deer for a while to get rid of them.

I deeply sympathize with Canada in her butter shortage. Maybe she will have to get around to the manufacture of margarine yet. It really isn't so bad.

Thanks for the paragraph, Pop. I'm glad to see you still can write. If I need any money I will cable, but I won't unless something unexpected happens. I still have the £20 in the bank. My leave at Oxford didn't cost anything. We lived in the college, I got a warrant for transportation, and there

---

[16] Special Police

were lots of men to spend money for my entertainment. Actually, there is a charge for the course, but the Canadian Legion pays it for Canadians. Doris and I are still going to Scotland—probably in February or March.

Must go to bed now, will finish this tomorrow.

Monday night

. . .

Tonight we came home for supper. As a reward for all my industry over the weekend all I have to do is put up my hair, & I can go to bed early. Tomorrow night the girls in our directorate are all going out for dinner to a Chinese restaurant.

I hope you are getting all my mail. Apparently both Marg & Blanche have sent parcels I haven't got. The last parcel I got from you had the pyjamas in it that you made.

Well, must sign off now and do my Philosophy homework.

Lots of love,

Teddy.

Tuesday, Nov. 7/44.

Dear Blanche:

So sorry I didn't get you written to over the weekend. I didn't get a letter from you last week, and none this week so far.

Had quite a nice week. Monday night stayed in, Tuesday night Doris and I went to a show, Wednesday night I went to class as usual, Thursday night Doris' brother-in-law was in town and we went out to supper with him, and then home. Carl and a pal of his were waiting for us when we arrived. After cooking the boys supper, the whole gang of us went to the pub, and when we came home went up to May and Kay's room for tea. Jim was in bed, and we went and knocked at his door every two minutes so he couldn't get to sleep, since he wouldn't get up. When we finally went down to our own room we discovered our bed-clothes all over the place—Jim had tried to get his own back. We haven't let on yet that we even noticed it. Friday night Doris went back to Leeds with Larry. I almost went, but didn't feel like going when I wasn't ready. Doris wasn't ready either, but she went. I was on a 48, but had a very lazy time—didn't do a thing. Saturday I cleaned the room and went out shopping before the stores closed. Saturday afternoon I did my laundry. At night Mac and I went out to the pub for a little while, then sat and talked until he went up to go to bed, then I read a while and went to bed, too. Sunday I got up about 12, did my ironing, washed my hair, took a bath, did my shining, and read.

I got Christmas presents. I will send Mom's and Dad's to Kenny at the company, also Dorothy and Dave's. I will send yours to you, and hope it gets there before Jan. 1st, if you leave then. Don't expect it wrapped.

Wednesday

I got a letter from you this morning, dated October 22nd. However I have not received the birthday parcel—none of them. Mail is piled up to the ceiling at Base Post Office. Heaven knows what will happen when the Christmas mail starts coming in. Maybe I'll have the birthday parcels by then. I think you can send me V-mail.[17] I get air-mail from home in good time. Marg got one from me in 7 days.

No, I think I would rather you didn't give the Colonel my telephone number. No matter what you say, the English are terribly rank-conscious, and maybe I would be more embarrassed then he would be. Anyway, I bet he wouldn't cook pancakes like our Canadian Colonel did.

Oh, the war was pushed out of the front headlines by the American election results this morning. Of course, the finals weren't in by this morning, but a guess a good enough indication. A gang of Americans stayed up at the Rainbow club all night (American Red Cross) to keep up with it.

I hope my letter with the Oxford Odyssey hasn't got lost, because I sure would hate to have to write all that again. Thursday night one of the Oxford left-overs (a soldier stationed at Camp Borden) phoned me wanting me to go out, but I am going out this Saturday with him, since we had company Thursday.

I think I have not received one box of chocolates. I got one box from somebody at Holton Avenue, Hamilton, and one box from Elbow. Didn't you mention that you had sent a box in between those?

Married girls over here are being threatened with being sent home. Most of them are very unhappy about it. Most of us talk about ice cream and steaks and decent coffee, and why we'd give anything to be home, but when it comes down to the final thing nearly everybody wants to see it through. My guess is that I'll make it next summer or fall.

Now that the ban is off London, I wrote Reimer and asked him to come up, but haven't heard from him. I wrote everybody else and asked them, too, and ten to one they'll all come the same weekend. Got a letter and a snap from a chap I met on the train to Lachine, so I answered, and I got a letter back right quick, saying that a real nice friend of his was coming to London and he gave him my phone number, would I entertain him. I will if he turns up.

I really must sign off now. Take good care of your tummy, and let me know if you are going back to Canada and if so, where to.

Lots of love,
Edna.

P.S. Have you got a snap of yourself you could send? The girls in the office want to see what you look like. They feel cheated if I don't read them your letters regularly.

---

[17] The same as an air mail.

Historical Note: The 1944 U.S. presidential election saw President Franklin Delano Roosevelt of the Democratic Party win the race for the White House over Thomas Dewey, of the Republicans, for an unprecedented fourth term and with more than fifty per cent of the popular vote. However, Roosevelt was in poor health, and died less than six months later, on April 12, 1945.

Monday, Nov. 13/44.

Dear Mom & Dad:

Just got your Air Mail of the 1st, and letters of the 22nd and 29th. I am sorry to report I haven't had my birthday parcels, but got one mailed Oct. 6 on Friday. Thanks a lot for the butter, it was perfect, and the cookies were swell. I haven't had any birthday parcels (Blanche & Marg also sent one) but still have hopes. Baldy phoned up Friday night to tell me he's now a corporal, I guess. He said base post office was a terrible mess, and I expect they're sorting from the top of the pile, and mine will be in the bottom.

Thanks for the Oxo cubes, but forget about having a soda biscuit with it—they just don't exist. I also wish I could describe English bread, but it beats even me.

Believe it or not I got a woollen <u>vest</u> out of equipment and wear it. Next week I am also getting some woollen pants. We have parade every morning. It's too bad Dad doesn't at least [illegible—holes in airmail paper].

I sent Christmas presents for you to Kenny, so hope he gets them to you on time.

Don't bother buying a place at the Coast for me to go to—just give me a hunk of Saskatchewan dirt. Besides, maybe I wouldn't like the coast. I haven't decided yet what I'm going to do, but am seriously thinking about it.

Oh yes, I meant to tell you about the V2. The minute Churchill admitted we had had them in London the papers made a great to do about them. They are rather weird, since you don't know when they're coming, but there aren't so many of them. Last night was the closest one. Doris was in the tub when we hear this roar, and she was down in about 2 seconds, shaking like a leaf. It didn't explode—we just heard this roar through the air, and hitting something. However, they can only send a few and they are getting closed in on all the time.

Listen, Pop, do you think I could learn to run the farm for you? I don't see why I couldn't. I can swear well enough now. As far as University goes, I still want to go, but if you decide you want me to stay home I don't think I'd mind.

Well, must sign off and do the dishes. I was glad to get your 3 letters at once since I hadn't heard from you for a couple of weeks. Also got a letter from Blanche. And a letter with a snap that an American took of me at Stratford. Will send it to you in my next letter. Lots of love, so long for now,

Love,
Teddy.

Nov. 19/44.

Dear Blanche:

    Sorry I didn't get you written to last weekend, but I usually depend on getting my letter to you done before 9 o'clock in the morning, or a few minutes at noon, and I was too busy this week. I got a letter from you last week, I think the date was Oct. 30th.

    I'm so glad Mr. Dalgleish approved of me. However, we don't "rough it." We just live Bohemian style—he's lucky he didn't sit on the floor. In our room we have French windows with a window at each side, large chest of drawers, small buffet, fireplace, small book-case, two small wardrobes, two day-beds, sink, small table under a window, two wicker arm-chairs, two straight chairs, fairly small table we use when we have company. The house is on a slope and the front is quite underground, but at the back where we are, it is at ground level and we have a kind of court that is in the centre of the block with houses all around. There is a nice lawn and trees, and fairly private since you can't get to it from the street—only through the houses.

    No, I don't think I have lost any weight either. I did when I first came, but am up on it now (so much starch). Our hobby is hunting up restaurants where you can get steaks, so therefore we have a good meal quite often. On top of that, we cook our own supper about 3 nights a week, so they are always good. Our meat ration allows us to have meat for two meals a week. We don't frequent the big classy restaurants. They charge the ceiling prices—5 shillings—and have terrible food, usually a choice of plain spam or fancy spam. The small, dirty dives serve good meals—usually black market steaks—and seldom charge over 4 shillings. We go to a place near Piccadilly where they have white table-cloths, waiters in tails, and steak. It is small and quite out-of-the-way, and the whole meal, including soup and coffee, only costs 5/. The big places start at 5/ then add 6d. for soup, 9d. for dessert, and anywhere up to a shilling for coffee. And English coffee—phew!—it's simply awful! It's not rationed, either.

    WOI Kelly, a friend of Midge's, is in town on leave, and he insists on taking all 3 of us out for lunch. We had lunch with him twice last week. Friday it poured rain all day, so at noon he was waiting for us with a taxi. We scooted down to the Quality Inn on Leicester Square. It is run by an American and is quite a civilized style. We had a marvellous lunch—<u>real</u> apple pie and cream.

    Friday night it was still raining and Kelly again had a taxi, we went to the Stage Door Canteen where our super dance orchestra, The Streamliners, were playing. We waited till they finished, then brought one of the boys home. He plays the bass violin, and is a real scream.

    I didn't go to class Wednesday night because I had a darned sore chest and back. I came home & went to bed—blankets, aspirins, hot tea, hot water bottle and mustard plaster on chest & back. After all that trouble I didn't feel a bit different in the morning, but eventually it got better.

Last Saturday a boy I know came in from Camp Borden and a gang of us went out. Baldy McLean phoned last week to tell me he was now a corporal.

I got the bath-salts on Thursday. Thanks a lot—the bubbles are weak-kneed, but they soften the water. In all the cities I've been in, London has the hardest water of them all.

I got a parcel from Marg last week—all Aylmer canned goods. Quite a treat—there were pears, peaches, tomato juice, soup, corn & chicken.

They are starting to send the W.D.'s home, and nearly anybody can go for the asking. I haven't asked—I think we'll be sent home next Spring anyway.

I bought you something real cute a long time ago, but when I started to look for it to send it for Christmas I couldn't find it. I'm sending you something else, although I'm afraid it will be late. When I pack to go home I'll probably find the original and bring it to you. It is a bracelet made of threepenny bits.

Rita (a girl in our office) wants to know the results of the Aviation Commission meeting.

We didn't go out at all over the weekend. We had four boys in for a black-jack game (guys who live in the house) Saturday night, and 3 in Sunday night. I lost about 2 shillings. There are now 11 Canadians in our house. What a place!

Thanks for the film—the 620 fits Mac's camera, and one of the girls in the office has a 120. Will try and take some good pictures and send you copies.

Must sign off now—I got your parcel away.
Love
Edna.

Nov. 20/44.

Dear Mom & Dad:

Well, the beginning of another week.

I got two parcels last week—I guess they were birthday parcels. Bath salts and film from Blanche, and a box of Aylmer canned goods from Marg. I think that must be the one she sent through Eaton's.

The first of the week was rainy and quite cold, but the end of the week was real warm and muggy. It seems funny to be November.

Wednesday night I didn't go to class since I felt I was catching cold, and it always seems twice as damp down in Lambeth. I went to bed instead, and caught the cold in bed.

A WOI friend of Midge's was in town last week and we went out a couple of days for lunch with him. Friday night we went to the Stage Door Canteen. Our dance orchestra was playing there. Tuesday night Doris and I went to a show. We stayed in all weekend. Did our washing & ironing, and I washed my hair. We played black-jack with the boys Sat. & Sunday nights. There are now 4 R.C.A.F. boys in the house as well as the 3 Army boys and we 4 W.D.'s. Quite a house, eh? Mr. Dalgleish told Blanche I was "roughing it" where I lived. I wrote her back right smart that we lived Bohemian style.

This week I got a snap sent to me that an American took of Kay Lewis and I in front of Shakespeare's birthplace. I will send it to you when I write—don't lose it, since I haven't got the negative.

I worked hard all last week, but not too hard today, although I'm all pooped out.

There was a lot of excitement here last week—a few restaurants started making ice cream again—out of powdered milk. Quite a treat, although I haven't had any yet.

If you ever see any prepared ice-cream powder send me some—I'll get Mrs. Roe to make it up.

Well, there really isn't a great deal to say. Everything is going along all right. The weather doesn't agree with me particularly—think I'll ask for a posting to the tropics.

Take care of yourselves, and have a nice holiday. I suppose you'll be getting away soon, and you should, too.

Lots of love for now,
Teddy.

Nov. 27

Dear Mom & Dad:

How are things going? I suppose you are still on the farm, but guess this will probably follow you all over Canada, nearly. I do hope you have some address to give the P.O. at Elbow. Got your letter dated Nov. 12th on Saturday. Yes, people are starting to drift home—the ones who have been here for 3 years, and they are also starting to let the boys go back after 1 tour of ops.

Holy smoke! You thinking about getting a flat (pardon me, suite). Are you going to settle down at the coast? I'm going to be home to help Dad run the farm next summer, and I'm going to get a real dog, meaning a big one, so tell Georgie he can have Trixie.

Our house gets crazier and crazier. There are now 14 Canadians in it, 3 came Saturday and I haven't seen them yet.

Last Tuesday a chap I met at Oxford called me up. He was in town on leave. He had a friend, so I took Doris and we all went to a dance. They are F.O.'s with the D.F.C.[18] The friend is cute, and said he came from Saskatoon, so I said lived on Avenue H, and did a bit of scratching of memory to describe. (Wouldn't Dad pick the Negro section of town to own houses in!) Finally I admitted I was from Elbow, and it turns out he knows more Elbow

---

[18] Distinguished Flying Cross

people than I do. He used to live at Lucky Lake, is the Heals' cousin, and used to visit Elbow all the time. His name is Glen Bassett. It's a small world. A boy from Wynyard lives at our house, too. He was posted to London for the hockey team. They play every Sunday morning at 9:30, away out of town. Needless to say, the whole house has to get up and go. I wouldn't Sunday morning, but I might as well have because they woke me up thoroughly. I will next Sunday.

Wednesday night I went to class, Thursday and Friday nights we stayed in. Oh no, Friday we went to a show. It was English-made, but very good.

Saturday we rushed home without dinner and went to the dog races (greyhound) with Mac. We met Jim out there with two Americans. We bet on every race, and I lost on every one except the last one, where I picked a long shot. I still ended up in the hole, though. There can't be anything equivalent to the dog races in Canada. I can't describe it all, but the most outstanding thing to me were the bookmakers with their bag of money and their board they chalked up the odds on—they change every time someone lays a bet with them. There are two men to each stand—one takes the money, the other spends his time signalling wildly with most weird gestures to a buddy away across the track.

Girls come out and walk the dogs around the track before each race—each race has a different set of dogs. I can't see why they run—surely after the first few times they catch on that they never catch the rabbit. Afterwards the Americans left, and we went home, picked up a couple more boys from the house and went out for a spaghetti supper. Doris and I were starved since we didn't have supper Friday or dinner Saturday. We played cards a while Saturday night.

I got up about 10:30 Sunday. The gang came in for their breakfast about 12. I did my laundry and rubbed my knuckles raw. The Sally Ann won't take girls' laundry anymore, so until we find a new one we do our own. We had a free-for-all in Jim's room and made a mess of it, but that's O.K.—he wasn't in.

Do you think there's going to be a civil war in Canada? If there isn't now, there will be when the boys get home. If people only knew what our boys on the continent put up with because there aren't any reinforcements, they'd chase the Zombies out of the country. It's going to be interesting to see what happens, anyway.

Well must sign off, now. Take care of yourselves—
Love
Teddy.

Nick was just a guy in the house. And Midge didn't live in the house; she was a friend of either May or Kay's. But she did work at Headquarters.

Historical Note: During World War II, "Zombie" was Canadian slang for a conscript.

Conscription, or compulsory military service, has been a contentious issue in Canadian military history, dividing Canada along French-English lines in both World Wars. At the outbreak of the Second World War in 1939, Prime Minister Mackenzie King, fearful of how the issue had threatened national unity in 1917 and brought about the downfall of the Conservative government of the day, promised "conscription if necessary, but not necessarily conscription." This led to the *National Resources Mobilization Act* which, in 1940, called for the national registration of all eligible men and women for domestic defence—not overseas duty. However, by the fall of 1944, it became clear that the Canadian Army needed infantry reinforcements to ensure the successful liberation of Europe that had begun with the Normandy Invasion. Conscription had finally become necessary, and King authorized the sending of 12,000 conscripts overseas in the last months of the war.

Nov. 28

Dear Blanche:

As Reimer says, "Tempus Fugit," and I can't figure out where November has gone. Got your letter of Nov. 14th last week. Even though it was Air Mail it arrived after your letter of the week before—right in order.

What a day—my boss is out with some plywood visitors from Canada, the Winco is out with an A.V.M.[19] from Canada and Holman is out snooping around the country. I have exhausted every possible job by now.

If the Y workers are the same as they used to be, they run a hostel or a camp and their chief duty consists of making sandwiches . . .

. . . I was at the Stage Door Canteen here. Its quite nice but not sumptuous . . .

Yes, I would take a job in England if I wanted to see it as badly as you do, and I don't think there's a nicer spot in which to work (than Cam.). Incidentally, the last weekend I was up there I entertained the two little daughters of a manager of Pie Radio who were visiting the Roes.

. . .

The A.F. gave us 5 free Air Mails for Christmas. Darned white, eh?

I darned near jumped off my chair (or got blown off) Sat. morning. A you-know-what landed about a block and a half from here. That's close enough.

Must sign off.
Love
Edna.

I worked in the engineering section of the Directorate of Air Services, and we often had aeronautical engineers—or "plywood" visitors—coming through the office.

[19] Air Vice Marshall

In the engineering section, we were responsible for transferring secret blueprints from the Ministry of Aircraft Production to Air Force Headquarters in Ottawa. Our bosses were all aircraft engineers who went around the country visiting factories and assembly plants in England, then would come back to make their reports to Canada. I worked primarily as a stenographer, but had other duties as well on occasion.

December 4, 1944.

Dear Mom & Dad:

How is every little thing this week? I wonder where you have got yourselves to. It sure seems hard to believe it is December.

The week has been very ordinary. Wednesday I went to class. They would choose that night to have the Headquarters dance, so I promised the gang I would go. I arrived at 10:30, was hungry since I hadn't any supper, got a sandwich at the canteen, and went to find the dance floor and the gang. Having found both, Mac and Bert tossed to see who would dance with me because, much to my horror, it was the last dance. I had it with Mac. We finally collected the gang to come home together. It took from 11 to 11:30 for everybody to get their coats, and that half hour was worth going for. I stood out in the hall (as did 500 other people), and saw more people I hadn't seen for ages than a few. Old Jarvis people that I knew were over here, but never knew where. I saw at least a dozen, and even though I couldn't remember all their names, it's funny how they remembered mine.

Thursday night I did my laundry, Friday night I ironed and got ready to go away Saturday.

Saturday afternoon Kay Lewis and I went to Canterbury. Look at a map, and you'll see it down in Kent, almost in the corner opposite Belgium. It's a beautiful county—the train ran quite a ways along the Thames Estuary, which is sea to me. It is fruit country, and the orchards run right down to the water. You can just see how lovely it would be in the summer. There were flowers out, and the grass is green, but the fruit trees were all black. Canterbury is a nice city—about 35,000 I think. It is old—old winding streets, old buildings, etc. We stayed at a place that Welfare got the name for us. It was about a mile from the centre of town, but very nice. A man and his wife and two little boys. We had lovely meals, and Sunday morning we had a real <u>egg</u> for breakfast— they had a part share in some chickens. We arrived Saturday about 6 o'clock, had tea and went back downtown to a show. We went back to the house, had a supper and went to bed. Sunday morning we got up about 9, had breakfast and went to a service in the Cathedral. After that, we went about the town, took some pictures (although it was almost raining), looked at St. Augustine's college, and the ruins of St. Augustine's Abbey. It is very old, dating back to about 1000. One part is a little church. We had our pictures taken in that— there is just one wall of it, and the rest of the ruins there is just the foundations of the walls. They are going to excavate it after the war. St. Augustine's college is still standing. It has been damaged by bombs, but was used right up until last year to train missionaries for such wild places as Canada.

We went back for dinner, then packed our bags and took them to the station, then went back to have a good look at the Cathedral. It is very large, and very lovely. It has been damaged some by bombs, but not too badly. By the time we had tea, we went to the station to get a train. We wanted to get the 6 o'clock because we didn't want to get home too late. Boy, were we tired. My legs still ached Monday. We must have walked miles and miles, but thought it was worth it.

The weather has been quite nice here. Chrysanthemums are still out—they must stay out all winter.

Wednesday 6th

Sorry I didn't get this away. Got your letter of Nov. 19th yesterday. Running down to Ontario for a couple of weeks—of all the gad-abouts! Your travelling stomach must have improved. Dad probably went with you in the end.

I got the parcel with my scarf in it. I thought I had mentioned it. That's the last one I got. You mentioned sending Blanche Christmas cake—I hope you sent me some. While I think of it—who addresses the parcels for you? I think you did the last one, but that is the first time. Whoever does spells Johnson wrong.

Yes, married girls are going home, but need I remind you I am not married. I'll be home next summer. They have enough air crew now, so they stopped training in Canada, so they don't need as big a staff. They are making the last trainees re-muster to ground, and in that way will have lots.

Doris is going home—if she weren't married she'd be going anyway—she has terrible headaches which the M.O. says is nerves.

As near as I can see they had better keep the Zombies at home, because if they ever got in the front line they'd get shot—from bullets going the wrong way. I do feel sorry that they don't like to be so far from home, away out in B.C. You don't hear the boys in Italy squawk because they haven't a soft bed—they're lucky if they have time to lie on the ground. And how about our boys on the Continent who are still wearing the same battledress they went over in in June? By the way, Barney is in Holland. They were resting up, but as you see in the news they're back in action now.

I sent Christmas presents for you and Dad to Kenny, you can pick them up when at Calgary—if they arrived.

Must sign off and get to work.

Lots of love,

Teddy.

Dec. 6

Dear Blanche:

Got your letter of Nov. 20th last week, and got the parcel this morning. Thanks so much. I'll not open the wrapped-up oddities, but we sampled the fudge at the office, and after many exclamations I am forced to admit that you can make fudge even if you can't cook. Oh yes, and thanks for the nuts, I'll endeavor to save them for Christmas. Mrs. Roe wanted me to go up, but we can't travel that week.

We just got tickets to hear the Royal Choral Society do the Messiah in Albert Hall on Dec. 30th.

. . .

Thursday

Taking my half-day shopping day this afternoon so must finish this and get it mailed. We are going to Harrod's, but probably won't buy much.

Will write this weekend since I am staying home.

Much love,

Edna

Dec. 12/44.

Dear Mom & Dad:

I don't know where the time has gone, but it's awful hard to realize it's just two weeks to Christmas.

If I had known that Dad would be in Moose Jaw and you down East[20] I would have written to him separately, but there's probably no use now, as I suppose by the time you get this you'll be at the coast. Give my love to Dorothy, tell her I keep trying to get time to write. I sent her a parcel. Also ask Grandpa if there's any place he wants me to look at for him, or anybody he wants me to look up.

Doris and I are getting New Year's holiday (4 days). We have Christmas Day and Sunday off as well, though. We can't travel at Xmas but can at New Year's, so we are going to Edinburgh. She is on leave now and has gone up there for a couple of days. She will be going home early in January.

. . .

Noon hour

I got two parcels this morning. The slippers are really cute, and fit. Everything looks swell. I don't know how you got the time to collect everything. I know how hard it is to find things nowadays. Thanks loads.

Must sign off now so this will get posted today.

Love,

Teddy.

---

[20] Mom had relatives in Ontario that she would visit on occasion.

Just to keep things straight for the following letter, there were two Berts: French Bert, a young kid in the air force who lived in our house for a short time, and Bert Wilson. However, after French Bert left, he came back to our local, the Crown and Sceptre.

Bert Wilson and I had met in Oxford, but I obviously made a bigger impression on him than he did on me at the time. Anyway, a couple of weeks later, he came up to London and he appeared at our door. We went out with the gang that night, and it got to be a bit of a habit. Things just kind of clicked. Bert was stationed at Camp Borden, near Aldershot, where he served with the Royal Canadian Ordnance Corps keeping track of inventory, so it wasn't too difficult for him to come up to London, with or without permission. There was always a spare room for him to stay in at the house. In fact, when I'd get home, Mrs. MacLean would often say, "Where have you been? Bert's been waiting for you!"

Bert and Edna (plus two others) in front of the dining hall at Balliol College, Oxford, October 1944.

Dec. 13/44.

Dear Blanche:

Haven't heard from you since I wrote last week. We have been sitting here in the office looking at the fog and talking about skating and skiing.

Went to class Wednesday night. Didn't do much else the rest of the week. Saturday afternoon I went to the Sadler's Wells Opera. It was two short ones— Gianni Schichi and Il Tobarro by Puccini. They were good. Saturday night Doris and I went with Mac to Bertorelli's—the spaghetti joint. Doris and a couple of the boys went to the show, and five of the boys and I settled down to a black-jack game in our room. I was up 2/6 once, and ended the game 5 pence up, which is good considering that I usually lose. The whole gang came trooping in between 10:30 and 11, and we made coffee and had crackers for the gang. We had quite a room full.

Sunday morning Nick woke us up at 7 o'clock to go to the hockey game. We arrived at Knightsbridge and had to wait for the truck, but finally it came, and the two teams and Doris and I set out for the rink at Croydon. We were playing 418 squadron, and it was some mix-up. We had to lend them two men and our goalie—the pro Johnny Bowers, who used to belong to Detroit. One of the men we loaned to 418 accidentally sat on Bowers so, of course, he couldn't get up and one of the men who was bona fide on our team got in a goal. The goalie we had didn't even have skates on. Our time was cut short because we were late. We went home and had breakfast, they cleaned up the room. In the midst of trying to shake mats under people's feet, and sweeping around them, who should arrive but Baldy MacLean. Then Bert Wilson arrived (a chap I met at Oxford). We just sat around and gabbed, and Baldy had to leave to go on duty at 5 o'clock. I went out for supper with Bert and a couple of boys from the house. Then Bert had to leave to catch his train back to camp, and I pressed my uniform and finally got to bed. Altogether it was quite a hectic weekend.

Monday night I went to "The Barber of Seville" by Sadler's Wells. I didn't like the leading lady—I had seen her once before. She has funny teeth and sings through her mouth. Also she sings opera with the gestures of a torch song. The romantic lead was nice looking and had a good voice but had a beer belly. Figaro was good though, and did the song "Figaro" awfully well. I arrived home about 10, starched some collars and went to bed. Last night I didn't do much constructive.

Doris went on leave Monday morning. She is going to Edinburgh and stopping at Leeds on the way back. We are both getting New Year's leave and going to Edinburgh. I'm going to get to that place if it's the last thing I do. We can't travel over Christmas, but can over New Year's.

There seems to be quite a lot in view for the week before Christmas, so I am sure we will have a good time. We won't have to work Christmas day, and will have Saturday afternoon, Sunday, and Monday, as well as our four days at New Year's. Half the staff will be off over Christmas Saturday morning and Boxing Day.

I don't know whether I ever told you about the theatres over here, but they have no comparison at home. The Theatre is a large industry in London, because everybody goes, and there are practically dozens of good stage plays on in the winter. Seats go at different prices, and at Sadler's Wells you can get anything from 10/ in the front stalls to 1/ gallery. They usually have several cloakrooms, and you leave your coat and bundles, hoping to heaven you find the right one again. The usherette will sell you a program and take your order if you want tea at the intermission. As soon as the curtain comes down on the first act, they are posed [sic] at the door and leap out from behind the curtains with a tea tray on each arm. You can also get coffee from a girl who carries around a coffee pot and milk jug, but most people know better. It didn't take me long to learn never to order coffee. Most theatres you can smoke in, but of course don't allow it in the stalls, on account of the actors' voices. Well, the curtain goes up on the second act to the tune of clinking tea-cups—people hurriedly putting the cups under their seats. In between the second and third act people don't know what to do, seeing most of them are full of tea, so they go down to the bar and swill quickly, trying to see how much they can drink in the interval; or else they climb over rows of people to visit someone they know. Oh it's a very chummy institution, is the Theatre. At the end, when people are impatiently wanting to get out, the cast all crowd on the stage, and as long as one person beats one hand on the other, the curtain will go up and down, and there they are, all smiling and bowing. However, if you can take the theatre in your stride you can see a lot of good plays. A new one of Noel Coward's is on—not new, I mean it has just started playing—Private Lives. I must try to get to it, but tickets are still hard to get.

I got a parcel last week from Mildred[21]—it was sure swell. May made some short-bread to put in. Also got a parcel from Barbara Bolton who used to be at Jarvis with me. It was swell—combs, washcloths, hand-cream, tooth-powder, tooth-brush, etc. and a pair of dark silk stockings. I also got a parcel of cookies from Minnie Mindorff (also from Jarvis). I thought it was swell of the kids, and I was sure surprised. Joyce sent me some clothes, two parcels, but I never got them, and have given up hope.

Also, angel, I haven't got the money from you yet. How on earth did you send it? I got my hair cut off quite short, and by doing it up each night, it manages to stay quite nice. The kids like it anyway.

12 o'clock

Just got your letter of Nov. 26th and pictures. Pauline said she didn't expect you to look like that, and Gwen said you are just as she pictured you.

The class I attend is Philosophy, run at Morley College (a night school) by the U. of London. Dr. Lewis from the U. is the lecturer, but we do not follow their syllabus. It is just a general course, with no credits, but I'll be able to take first-year Philosophy like a breeze, and one credit is practically in the gab. Of course, this way will probably spoil the interest of the class.

I got two parcels from Mom yesterday. There is Xmas cake, cookies, butter, bars, etc. and a pair of seal-skin slippers just like I wanted.

Married women here are going home, they expect, in January. Replacements came in this week—more kids from Canada. Thrilled because I bet they didn't expect to get over now. That means, of course, that Doris will be going.

I can't understand the High Commissioner letting you sit around until now without snapping you up. By the way, who is he?

I am just pining for some really nice civilian clothes. Maybe I ought to go home. We had a half day off for shopping, and Doris and I each bought a hat. That raised our morale. I have another wretched cold, partly on my chest. However, I have been for several months without one. I can't understand it—I take my halibut oil capsules. Doris and I both take them religiously at breakfast.

[21] Mildred was a good friend of my sister Blanche. She was a character.

Am enclosing a tit-bit about tubes to see which you would rather, ride in or walk. Must sign off now. Got an air mail from Mom, during the course of which she changed her mind three times about going East, and ended it in the mood to go, but don't really know if she did or not. I should think the Coast would satisfy her, seeing she's not a good traveller. She wants me to make up my mind to go to Saskatoon U. so she and Dad can just go there in the winter, and stop travelling in the cold. I don't know what to do, but guess I'll have all winter to decide.

So long for now,
Love,
Edna.

I had started university before the war and completed one year at Regina College, taking general courses: French, History, Biology, Chemistry and Home Economics. I failed Home Economics, so it became a running joke with my family that not only did I set up housekeeping in London, but I actually did it quite well. Although I never returned to university, I had every intention of doing so, and thought the philosophy course I took at the University of London would help my future studies.

December 18/44.

Dear Blanche:

I received your Air Mail from Mt. Brydges. How nice to be able to take sick leave when you want, or do you just stay sick all the time in case you want leave? Anyway, it's nice to be able to see Mom—she'll be seeing all the family in December by the time she has the rounds made.

Got two parcels from Mom last week—or did I tell you?

Here is my story of the Lafayette Hotel in Windsor. Joyce and I stayed there on our way back from New York. After much wrangling we got a room and when we went to it (finding it ourselves) discovered there were no sheets on the beds. After not less than three calls to the desk, a woman finally brought up some sheets, and after another one, brought up some towels. Dead tired as we were, we set to and made our beds. Then, about 7 o'clock in the morning, somebody started banging on the wall right outside the door, and a man was standing on a ladder at our transom painting, and shouting to somebody at the other end of the hall. Nice restful place.

I hope Grandpa is alright. You didn't mention whether Carl was at home. The last time I saw him, in November, he expected to be leaving right away.

Didn't do much this week—went to class, the last one for three weeks. Saturday afternoon I cleaned up the room, did my laundry, etc. Saturday night I wrote a letter, sat and gabbed. Sunday I did my ironing and had a good sleep-in. Baldy arrived at 1 o'clock when I was just doing the breakfast dishes. He came to get Paul (whom he knows) to go to the hospital to see somebody they both know. This Paul comes from Moose Jaw, but really lived at Riverhurst—his people just moved to M.J. His dad is an engineer on the Riverhurst water project. He tells me the water broke through to Caron this fall. Also had for company Sunday Nick's brother and friend from his hometown—Wynard. The brother is back—wounded in France—and had some interesting stories. You, of course, have heard about the company of the Winnipeg Rifles that went to surrender and 19 were shot. The sequel to that story is that reinforcements came and the Germans who did the shooting were taken prisoner. They tied them up and gave a guy from the company a rifle and said, "Go ahead, shoot them." "Nope," he said, he couldn't shoot them. He took the bullets out of the rifle, fixed a bayonet, and went to town. No wonder the Germans fear the Canadians—they're devils when they get going. I don't remember if I sent you a copy of the Zombie's Prayer[22] or not, but am enclosing one. Hope I don't get sent up for sending obscene literature through the mail.

Some of the stories we hear from the War Diaries are really good. Like one CWAC[23] company that didn't have anything to put in their diary, so put in official story about their Captain losing her button pants. Rita's sister is in the CWACs in Antwerp, and is having an interesting time. She has been there quite a while.

Doris is on leave and supposed to be back for this morning. When she didn't come back last night, I just thought she had decided to take another day's unofficial leave. However, the discips were down my neck this morning wanting to know where she was. After phoning the medical section to see if they had any word I, in desperation, called the house to see if she had phoned or wired there. There was a post-card stating that she had broken her arm—but didn't say where. I don't mean in the femur or the other side (whatever that is), but whether in Edinburgh or Leeds. The post-mark was indistinguishable, and also the thing was written with her left hand. Of all things to do. Usually all the good things happen to her, and all the bad to me. However, she will probably have a nice holiday.

. . .

I should think by this time you would have learned about the avidity of English stamp collectors and would have more consideration than to put your parcels through a post office meter. If we can keep the Winco from seeing the stamps, Kath, our civilian girl, gets the stamps.

I mailed you a copy of last week's "Wings Abroad" with a sketch of Bob Turnbull from Govan. There was write-up about him in the Canadian "Wings" last summer, when he was a Wing Commander.

---

[22] The Zombie's Prayer was not among the saved letters, and all attempts to find a copy were unsuccessful.
[23] Canadian Women's Army Corps

Doris and Edna in front of 55 Holland Road, after Doris broke her arm when visiting Edinburgh. She went home not long afterwards. December 1944.

Really must sign off, as I have to go. I don't know what Saunders has been doing all day—I haven't had any dictation yet.

By the way, my camera size is 620. I took a roll of film at Canterbury, and they turned out quite well. I will know a bit more how to handle it for future pictures. I got an F/O from Signals to develop them—at least Kay Lewis did—she went with me—he did two copies of them. I'd send home some of the snaps I have, but nobody stays put, and I'm afraid of them getting lost, and most of them I haven't got the negatives for.

Will write you on Monday or Tuesday to let you know what kind of Christmas I had.

The kids say to tell you they appreciated your artistic efforts in your last letter. The nerve of anyone to say you couldn't draw!

I must say that the weather so far hasn't been cold, but is terribly damp. However, I don't mind it. I have odd twinges of rheumatism, but my sinus doesn't bother me. We have a gas fire-place, and the way we hug that thing is cruel. First one out of bed lights it, and then we dress practically on top of it.

I don't know when Doris will come home—I should imagine she could travel this week. Hope she makes it for the weekend anyway. I am duty clerk to-night, but don't have to pull the black-outs now because black-out time comes before quitting time, so the boys pull their own.

Must stop now,—take care of yourself.

Love,

Edna.

My room-mate Doris went to Edinburgh for the weekend. She fell off a bus and broke her arm, and she swore that the "clippie" pushed her. A "clippie" was a tram conductress. She arrived back with arm set, but not right, so was sent home, as it wasn't healing. She was supposed to join her husband in New Zealand.

Doris and bus drivers didn't seem to get along. One morning we ran to try to catch the bus as it drove away. Doris then put a curse on the driver that when he got off the bus, his pants would fall down.

Staff of Directorate of Air Services;
Engineering in back row. Photo Credit: RCAF O/S HQ.

Engineering Division at the Directorate of Air Services.
Photo Credit: RCAF O/S HQ.

Dec. 28/44.

Dear Mom & Dad:

. . . Well, I must start to tell you about my Xmas festivities. It was as merry and as drunken as a bunch of crazy Canadians could make it.

Wednesday night we had our headquarters dance. I guess it was pretty good, but I just had a fair time. Thursday night was our Directorate party. We had it at the Connaught Rooms—a kind of banquet hall where you can rent rooms for parties. It was a straight cocktail party. Everybody got very high and called everybody else by their first names. Our bosses were supposed to meet their girlfriends at the Exhibition Club, so a gang of about 8 of us decided to go. My boss took a sign from outside the Connaught rooms, and I had to talk a cop out of putting us in jail and talk my boss into taking it back. After calling him a lot of names, which I hope he doesn't remember, we finally got on our way. After arguing our way into the Exhibition Club, one of the officers' girlfriends got mad and left. I don't see why—we were only an hour late. I have a hunch she resented the staff coming along. However, we had a good time without her. From there, 4 of us went to Pauline's flat where we had coffee. S/L Fishbourne, the intelligence officer, somehow got with us, and finally talked us into going home. (I have seen him several times since and he shouts, "Hi Johnny!" but I haven't the nerve to answer, "Hi, Tommy!")

Friday morning everybody was late, and polished shoes and buttons in the office. Of course the Winco waits until I'm doing a ballet dance with my shoes and tunic off to come in. We all quit early Friday afternoon. The people who took Christmas were off then, but I had to go to work Saturday morning. Friday night Mac and I went to get the makings of the Xmas dinner. It wasn't exactly black market stuff, but we paid extra. We got a goose and two chickens, apples, oranges and nuts and whiskey (the last 3 practically impossible to get ordinarily). Saturday afternoon I cleaned up the room and did laundry. Doris got back last Wednesday—with her right arm in a sling she's rather helpless, but getting better. She can practically dress herself now. You see I'm cook and nurse—never thought I had it in me. Day before yesterday she went out to our hospital and had a new cast put on.

Well, anyway to get back to Xmas, the boys peeled the potatoes and made the stuffing. I cooked the vegetables, set the table and organized people, since by that time of day everybody was everywhere. It was a real good dinner, if I do say so.

The things that were wrapped up in my parcels I saved until Xmas day to open. Got a blue taffeta slip from Marg, pants & nylon brassiere from Blanche, I think, powder & cream from Marg, and a book of Ogden Nash poems. Very nice altogether.

Boxing Day I had to go to work, but our office was terribly cold, and there was no mail and not a lot to do, so we quit at noon. Went home, and we went to a show. I had a terrible time getting to work—Boxing Day is quite a holiday, and there was just supposed to be Sunday bus service. On top of that there was fog and things were just crawling. We waited at the bus stop for a while and then got a ride to Hyde Park Corner in a fire truck—no, not a big red one with bells and ladders, just a little covered-in truck that belonged to the National Fire Service. We waited 15 minutes for a tube at Hyde Park and arrived in late, but then so did everyone else. It's been foggy all week, and sure is thick today.

We wrote a joint letter in the house and will send you a copy as soon as it comes off the press. Must get this away. Haven't written to Blanche yet, but at least I think I know where she is. Hope you got the Xmas present that I sent to Kenny. Waiting still to find out where you are.

Lots of Love,
Teddy.

The gang of 55 Holland Road, Kensington, in the courtyard, Christmas 1944.

Dec. 30/44.
Dear Blanche:

Will try and write this while the gang is out.

Didn't get a letter from you last week.

We had a very merry Christmas, all the gang here. We were set on having a good time, so we did. Had a nice Xmas dinner—goose and chicken & pudding, even oranges and nuts that Mac got through a little finagling. Of course we paid extra for them. The dinner, including the drinks we got in, came to £15 and something for 15 people. Maybe that sounds like a lot in American money, but it isn't much here.

Mr. Williams called me up last week and sent me a note in the mail. Thank you very much, dear—I shall do something useful with it. The old boy explained to me it was on Barclay's bank, and I said, "Oh, that's handy, that's my bank," and I could hear him swallowing his tonsils. I put my money there because there's one handy to headquarters.

Wednesday night we had an H.Q. dance, and what a brawl! It would have done credit to any Canadian dive. The whole gang from our house went, of course.

Thursday night was our Directorate party. It was a cocktail party in the Connaught Rooms. Everyone got stinking before they left. There were some pictures taken and I saw them yesterday. Everyone looks cross-eyed. About 8:30 two of our engineering officers, the intelligence officer, the F/Sgt. from Establishments and Pauline, Gwen and I went to the Exhibition Club. It wasn't much of a place—dance floor, etc. From there we went to Pauline's flat for coffee, dropping our two officers off with their girlfriends, who were rather peeved, I think. Finally, after much to-do, got home. Every time S/L Fishbourne sees me now he calls, "Hi, Johnny!" I almost, but not quite, answer, "Hi, Tommy!" I have also developed into Johnny for F/L Quinn, but not F/L Saunders. After me talking him out of the hands of a cop, too, who wanted him to either to replace a stolen sign or go to jail. Under pressure he returned the sign, mumbling all the time he'd rather wrap it around the cop's neck. We had Saturday afternoon, Sunday and Xmas day off. Christmas dinner was cooked under my able supervision (bow). Imagine me!

Some of the kids went to R.C. Midnight Mass Xmas Eve, then went to Protestant church Xmas morning. I didn't go to either.

Haven't really done much this week. Didn't work very hard. I have today, Sunday, Monday & Tuesday off. Not going anywhere since Doris can't travel and can't do enough for herself really to leave alone. She came back from Edinburgh a week ago Wednesday. Guess I told you she went there on leave and broke her right arm.

This afternoon we went to Albert Hall to hear "The Messiah" done by the Royal Choral Society and the London Symphony Orchestra. It was sure super. If you ever see "Love Story" advertised, go and see it. There are some good shots of Albert Hall and London in it. It's an English-made picture. Saw "Our Hearts were Young & Gay" last week. Sure got a kick out of those two American girls in London. Londoners wouldn't half appreciate it, I'm afraid.

Oh, thanks very much for the underwear. Got a slip from Marg, too, and a book of Ogden Nash poems. Oh, by the way, I didn't send the Zombies' Prayer—forgot it. Maybe you thought the censors liked it. By the way, some Zombies are here now, training. They go around in gangs. Had a letter and Flemish card from Elmer Knutson. He is also in Holland. Says he may get leave to England in January. Not unless things improve now, he won't. People make me sick when they think the war is over. It's just changing type of warfare—less aerial and more just plain slogging. They'll only win by weight of numbers. Mac has been re-boarded and put in a higher category, which means infantry for him. That's just one of things the boys have against the Zombies—Staff Sgt. to infantry private. Specialised tradesmen, too, are getting guns instead of tools shoved at them. They are recruiting thousands more women here. Everywhere you look now you see women in uniform.

Tell that to the people with their hands folded over their fat bellies, wondering why they don't hurry and make them new cars.

Really must sign off—I have to write to Joyce along with dozens of other people as usual. Cheerio—

Love

Edna.

Jan. 6/45.

Dear Mom & Dad:

Haven't had any mail from you for two weeks, but got 2 letters today—Dec. 15 & 21. Also 2 from Blanche, 1 from Marg, a Xmas card from Aunt Maud, and the cutest card from Al in France (he's just an American left over from the summer—haven't heard from him in ages).

Guess I must have told you before that it is really is right that Carl is going home—haven't heard from him in ages anyway.

My dear mother, goods isn't so scarce here—it's just that you have to have clothing coupons to get it (plus 100% luxury tax). Jack Woods donated me some of his coupons before he went to India, by putting up a fair story I managed to buy civilian clothes with them.

I wrote you last week about Xmas. I had a very quiet New Year's. Am enclosing a composite letter the gang here made up, and Mac got it mimeographed. Haven't done a thing all week. Worked just average. It continues to be cold but not as bad as last week.

I must tell you about a new labor-saving device we have invented. We have a wooden floor in our room with carpet in the middle and rug in front of the fire-place. One night I was sitting placidly on a chair when one side went down suddenly. I thought the chair had broken, but when I tried to move it discovered one leg had gone through the floor. We are on the bottom layer and I think there is nothing underneath it. We pulled the rug over the hole and it makes a wonderful spot for sweepings. We can put the dirt under the carpet indefinitely without making a bulge. That's the real way to keep house.

Doris doesn't have to go to the office—I guess she won't go to work again here. I looked a bit at rooms this afternoon but hate to leave here. I'll have to pay 32 shillings alone, but didn't see anything cheaper than that. The court at our back is so nice in warm weather, the gang here are swell, and Mrs. McLean is darned nice to us. If you see any nice little thing you think she'd like, how about sending it? Anything in the fabric line would be nice, since it all takes coupons and I think she uses hers on her son who goes to school up in Devon. A dish towel or two, hand towel, small tablecloth or pair of stockings (lisle).

Mr. Reid at Blanche's place always reminds her to buy my Life magazine every week. After our house reads them they go to the hospital and all the boys sure enjoy them.

Went to my class at Lambeth this week. Two alerts while I was there. Really the V2's are much less nerve-wracking than the V1's, because with the

V2's you carry on in blissful ignorance until one hits you, and with the V1's you know they are coming and have a nervous 5 or 10 minutes until you hear them go off someplace else.

I suppose you saw that Glenn Miller is missing. Too bad Frank Sinatra or Eddie Cantor wouldn't try the trip.

Took some pictures around Xmas. If they turn out will send you some.

Might be seeing Elmer Knutson this month, or maybe Barney. They're due for leave to England. Guess they'll be glad to get out of the lines.

Well, I haven't much to say—guess I'll sign off, and try to write to the rest of this damned family.

Lots of love,
Teddy.

Historical Notes: The V1 was superceded in September 1944 with the more terrifying, rocket-powered V2 bomb. Where the V1 warned Londoners with an ominous "putt-putt" sound before exploding, the V2 made no noise. Just a sudden blast as it hit the ground, leaving a huge crater, as well as destroying everything in the vicinity.

Glenn Miller (1904–44) was one of the most popular musicians and band leaders during the Swing Era, and his popularity only increased when he joined the U.S. Army in 1942. Captain Miller's mission was building morale, bringing a touch of home to the troops, and modernizing military music. Therefore, it was a terrible shock to all Allied troops when, on December 15, 1944, the plane he was on went missing during a flight from London to Paris, where he was to make arrangements for a Christmas broadcast. The plane and all who were on it were never found.

Jan. 15

Dear Mom & Dad:

Hope you have been having a nice holiday. I have written you regularly and hope you have been getting the mail. I didn't have a letter from you last week.

This week has been quite dull. Wednesday night I went to class, Thursday night Baldy McLean and Nicky came down. Saturday afternoon Doris came downtown and we went to the Hong Kong and had a Chinese dinner. Then we came home, had tea & Doris went to the show with Nick. I did a washing and ironing and washed and put up my hair, and finally got to bed about 12, after we finally shoved the boys home (we're getting so used to it now we have the urge to go to bed and leave the boys sitting there talking—I did one night).

Sunday was a nice day so we got up early (11 o'clock) had breakfast, dressed, polished and bathed and went downtown. We had our pictures taken at Leicester Square. I took a few snaps (Baldy gave me a film), went to a V1 exhibition, had tea in a Corner House (Lyons), then went to an "Amusement" place. Slot machines, rifle range, etc. We had a try at everything, then finally went home.

I have been quite busy at work—nearly came to blows with the Winco twice this week, and one of these days I'm really going to kick him in the shins.

My boss was off a couple of days with the 'flu. Doris hasn't got her movement order yet, but Mac has—to the infantry. Poor old Mac has to revert to a private.

Well, I had better get to work. Next weekend I am on a 48, but don't know where I am going.

As they say here—cheerio,
Love,
Teddy.

Jan. 23/45.

Dear Blanche:

Haven't heard from you for a couple of weeks. Got an air mail from mom today after a long silence. Haven't been doing anything terrifically exciting. Went to class Wednesday, stayed home Thursday. Friday a guy we know who is in the dance band came down to tell us about their trip to Belgium. He is a scream, & I gather had quite a bit of excitement—saw all the big January dog-fights; while on one station two Jerry paratroopers landed in American uniform, killed two Canadians & stole a jeep, but eventually got shot after roaring around the station. He brought us some perfume from Lille, which is sure strange-smelling stuff. He swears somebody pulled a swap on him and filled the bottles with petrol, but I don't think it smells that good. However, Art thinks it is very exotic smelling.

Saturday night Bert Wilson came to town. He was supposed to be just passing through on leave, but stayed till Sunday night. Saturday the gang of us went to the pub, Sunday afternoon we went to a show, then to Bertorelli's for supper.

It snowed some more over the weekend. What a thrill. I have some good snapshots of the snow in St. James's (pronounced Jameses, believe it or not) park, which I will send to you next week in an ordinary letter. You'll have to pass them on, since I have just one copy.

Last night Lorne Cecil (I used to go out with him at Jarvis) called up. Along with a friend of his we went to see "Constant Nymph" which has just arrived here & which I was disappointed in, then a Chinese supper at Hong Kong. Got home quite early. He is coming down Thursday night. He is stationed up north and is just in town on leave. What with the boys in the house, we do alright.

Mom says they bought a house and sold it to Dorothy and Dave. I have a few thoughts about that, which will look better unwritten. What makes me laugh is that Mom bought a bedroom suite so I could always have some place to sleep when I was there. I certainly hope she doesn't think I'm going to settle in there. Well, must sign off as you see.

Love,
Edna.

January 29, 1945.

Dear Mom, Dad, Dorothy, Dave & Georgie:

Received your Air Mail the first of the week, and an ordinary letter later on. Also received parcel from Dorothy on Friday. Thanks a lot. Everything was fine, except that the box was squashed, and had been re-wrapped at the post office, but nothing was squashed except the cake and we ate it anyway, and it was good. We had the tomato juice for breakfast, and also coffee with decent milk in it. The next time anybody sends a parcel, some decent coffee would be very much appreciated. Oh, yes, we both have a little head cold, and no Kleenex, so the T.P. was very welcome. You should see the sandpaper they hang up in the bathrooms here. Did I tell you, Mom, that I received the shirts and Lux?

Well, I am glad you got settled in a house. Maybe now Dad won't want to go back to the farm. Is he going to get the boat sent out?

Don't count too much on me being home next summer. The Air Force doesn't know yet that I'm going. Movement right now is very slow, although it may speed up. There are still a lot of married girls who haven't gone, and others who have asked.

Had a busy week last week. Monday with Cec, I went to the show. Tuesday, Paul and I and Doris and Jack (who happened to be there visiting) went to Pauline's flat to clean her gas heater. We had a nice quiet time, and Pauline made us lunch. Doris had just received a huge big cake from New Zealand, and we took half of that over. Wednesday night I was supposed to go to class, of course, but I was tired, and it was miserable out, and the thought of the trip fazed me, so I went home and did my laundry instead. Thursday night, Cec came down with a friend. We couldn't get any of the other girls to go to the dance, so Mel went with us on my assurance that there were lots of girls there, and there were, but I felt alright going to the dance with three boys. We all had a good time. . . .

Friday night it seemed to me I stayed home, catching a cold. Saturday morning I worked hard, and to top my misery the Winco told me to come back to work Sunday morning. . . . I went home and to bed feeling sorry for myself. However, Pauline phoned about 6 to say I didn't have to go in, so I got up, feeling much better, had something to eat (Doris had gone out) and started to do a laundry about 9:30. About 10 Doris came in. We sat in Art's room (we always hang out there when it is awfully cold because his room is small and warm), talking and cracking nuts all over his carpet until about 1 o'clock. Sunday we got up about 12, had a leisurely breakfast as usual. I did my ironing, and Doris got a cleaning spell. Holy smoke, nothing could stop her—she even washed the floor, which is something unheard of. We had dinner early, since she was going to the show with Nick. I washed my hair, put it up, did my shining, and had a bath, and mended lots of stockings. By this time I was ready to go to bed.

Gwen and Rita are members of the Churchill Club, so Thursday four of us went there for lunch. It was a club for the intelligentsia in peace time—school-teachers and the like, but now they have unbent to let Service people join, temporarily. They serve lunch and dinner for 2/6, which is very cheap, and it was a good lunch, too. I am going to join. It is in the cloisters of Westminster Abbey, in what was formerly a boys' school, I think. There is the dining room, cloakrooms, etc. Every week they have somebody really good to lecture. This week Michael Hambourg is forsaking the London Symphony Orchestra to give a recital. Later on in the month Alexander Korda[24] is lecturing, also Lord Vansitartt, and other notables.

Mac's transfer to the infantry was stopped, and he was still going to the Continent but as a clerk, but now that has been stopped—at least for three months. He is glad, but I think I would want to go. It was to second echelon. It's no picnic, but there are Canadian Army girls there, and I guess it would be safe enough for him. Rita's sister is over there, so we hear first-hand what is happening. At least in the social life of 2nd Echelon. They have instituted compulsory posting for A.T.S. to the Continent—up to now it has been voluntary, and they have had mixed ack-ack[25] batteries over for a long time.

Taking up all the news spread for the past week has been the Jones-Hulten murder case—the American soldier and girl who killed a taxi driver. Of all places he picked her up in Hammersmith—near us, which reminds us not pick up strange American soldiers, since they may be Chicago gunmen. They say there is a gang operating on the Continent that would put Al Capone to shame; all American soldiers who have taken advantage of the presence of tons of equipment and supplies and the impossibility of telling a murder or robbery from sniping or looting. Anyway, between the Russians and Betty Jones, the Allied activities have been pushed to the back page.

It sure has been cold here all week. Got to 2 below, which is as cold as 45 below, I swear it. The sea even froze along the edges. This puts a load on the fuel situation, which was strained before. If they would only build decent houses and put furnaces in them, they would discover they would save a lot of fuel and be warmer, instead of having a little coal grate or gas burner in each room. All of England goes around with a red nose all winter, and everyone seems to have a cold—even the English. I can't understand why they hung on to the country this long. I think I'll go to Bermuda when I get discharged, even if it is summer, so I can get warm and stay warm for a few days. All

---

[24] Alexander Korda (1893–1956) was a Hungarian filmmaker who gained international fame as a producer in Great Britain and the United States, and Lord Vansittart (1881–1957) was a noted British diplomat of the day. However, the reference to Michael Hambourg is probably incorrect. Although there was a famous musician of this name, he died in 1916. Michael Hambourg, however, had four sons, who also rose to prominence in the musical world, so maybe this concert featured one of them.

[25] Anti-aircraft fire.

kidding aside, I have planned what I am going to do the first summer holidays I have from U. I am going out to the West Coast and get a job on a boat going to Los Angeles. I should just have time to make the trip there and back. I can now cook, make beds, clean and scrub or, if absolutely necessary, act as steno. You don't need me on the farm in the summer, anyway, because this is slack time. However, if the worst comes to the worst, I can make the trip in one month, and work for you the other two months. But I think help will be plentiful by that time. You need somebody, anyway, because you can't run the house and cook for the men like you did last summer.

I sent some pictures to Blanche, and she will probably send them on to you or Kenny. Whoever they get to last had better hang on to them.

I am not going out tonight. Paul insists I do homework on Monday nights, since he needs company to study, and he is doing Physics, so I shall probably spend the evening reading Philosophy.

Must sign off now. Can't post this until tomorrow because I haven't your address here.[26] Tell Uncle Dave I am going to Scotland February 16th and will look up noted relative, since I am going to spend a day in Glasgow, although I intend to make Edinburgh my headquarters.

Good-bye for now.

Love,

Teddy.

(*over*)

Read over your letters when I got home.

I regret to say the cake was mouldy. I wasn't going to tell you. I think you should have taken it out of the can after it was cooked, to store it, then put it back in to send it.

Where is Dave working?

This will kill you—I'm going to get a kilt in Scotland. Lucky I don't belong to any clan—I can just pick out a pretty tartan.

Well, must sign off again and do a bit of studying.

Love again,

Teddy.

P.S. *Doris got her cast off and can't move her arm so she has gone to stay in the hospital, they told her for a month. Looks as if she won't get home for a while.*

Historical Note: Famously known as the Cleft Chin Murder Case, the sensational slaying of a London cabbie by American soldier Karl Hulten and British showgirl Elizabeth Maud Jones made the latter two household names—even beating out news of the war. The case inspired the 1989 Hollywood film, *Chicago Joe and the Showgirl*, starring Canadian actor Kiefer Sutherland.

[26] This letter was typewritten at work.

Feb. 2/45.

Dear Blanche:

I sent you some pictures last Monday. I fully intended to write a letter as well, but when it got to be Thursday and I still hadn't written I thought, "Why not merge two weeks in one," and I didn't need any coaxing.

I didn't get any mail from you this week—nor from Mom. It has been rotten.

I'm sorry I wasn't home when your man took the trouble to call twice, but you know how little time these popular girls have.

All the girls in the office read your letters—next step will be to let the officers in on them.

. . .

Uncle Dave sent me his niece's address in Glasgow. I'll phone her, I suppose, when I go up, but I'm darned if I like looking up relatives. I know I'd hate to have unknown nieces of my uncle pop in on me—I like to choose my friends. By the way, my leave starts on the 16th, I'm going to Dover for the weekend, then up to Edinburgh on Monday. It takes a whole day or night, but as there are no proper sleepers, naturally I like to travel by day. I imagine it will be pretty horrible—you don't get up and walk around when you get tired. If you could there wouldn't be any room anyway. If I don't get a letter written, I'll write a postcard.

Doris got her cast off and couldn't use her arm so she is now in the hospital, but her movement order came in (to go home) so they are letting her out next week.

Mac is not going in the infantry or to the continent now. They worked some kind of wrangle.

. . .

Our philosophy is going fine. We are now up to Kant, whom Dr. Lewis agrees with, for a change. Have you ever heard of Joad? He's a philosopher who kicks around London. Dr. Lewis has the utmost contempt for him—I think because Joad makes a business out of his philosophy.

I have been sitting by the gas-fire (as usual) and am now well done on all sides, so think I had better get mobile and get my hair up.

So long for now—

Love,

Edna.

P.S. The cigarettes arrived, but since we can now buy Canadian ones here, I had already sent Mr. Brunker a carton. Told him I'd get him more if he especially liked them.

It seemed that all of London got warm by gas heaters, supplied by some company to give you a measured amount of gas for a shilling. However, by November, you could hardly find a shilling. They were all in gas meters waiting to get collected.

Feb. 6/45.

Dear Mom & Dad:

I hear there has been a mail slow-up but I hope you have enough sense to know it is the mail and not to worry. I haven't heard from you for two weeks, but I don't worry because I haven't had any mail at all.

Right now I am in the theatre waiting for Noel Coward's "Private Lives" to start. Will let you know what it was like at the end of this. . . .

Saturday afternoon Rita and I went with Kath to her friend Muriel's to meet husband Ted and baby Stewart. We had a nice tea. Coming back I changed to a 49 bus at Shepherd's Bush and who should be on it but Bert Wilson. He had 'phoned 3 times, and decided I had to come home sometime. This was about 8:30. We went out to the pub. He stayed the night in Jim's bed. Mrs. MacLean has taken to him, smart boy. I made breakfast Sunday morning, or afternoon, we talked and since it was a nice day decided we had better not waste it, so went for a walk, then to the show. I got him to go back early (8:30) saying he needed sleep, because I was awfully tired myself.

A new man corporal came in to replace Gwen and we are having lots of fun breaking him in.

Had a hectic day today, and was duty clerk last night. We got in a new officer (which doesn't alter the amount of work, but Pauline is away on leave, which leaves me Quinn).

The play was very good, and really funny. Must get this posted, or you'll never get it.

Love,
Teddy.

Kath Butler was an English employee of the RCAF. She was our main help in dealing with things English and a good friend. She came to Canada to visit twice.

Feb. 24
[postcard showing The Forth Bridge from N.]
"We shall never stop, never weary, and never give in."
—The Prime Minister

Dear Folks:

Last weekend I was busy getting here and this weekend will be busy getting back, but will write the first of the week. Saw the Walls. Have travelled about and saw lots. Will tell you all about it. So long for now.

Love,
Teddy.

February 26/45.

Dear Folks:

First of all, don't kick at the carbon copy[27]—since I'm going to say the same things, don't see why I should write three individual letters, and this saves time.

I am still in the land of the living, although my feet keep wanting to dispute that. Honestly, we might as well have gone on a walking tour of Scotland, but that's the way to see things.

We left Saturday morning. It was a nice day, and since the scenery was all new, it didn't seem like a long trip. We left at 9:40 and arrived at Edinburgh at 6:30. We went straight to the Can. Legion for supper. While eating, a Merchant Navy kid came to ask us if we wanted to go to a party somebody was putting on and had asked the Legion to send some people. Since we didn't have a hotel room until Monday, we were staying at a private house and wanted to find it before we did anything, so we promised to come back after we had been there. By the time we had found it, and had chatted with the people and washed up, it was too late to go back, so we just sat and talked and finally went to bed. They were very nice—typical Scottish. The house was in the West end of Edinburgh, higher than the rest of the city, and very airy. From it we would see R.L. Stevenson's house, and two spans of the Firth Bridge.

Sunday we got up about 10:30 and, after having an egg (with shell on, like hens lay) for breakfast, we went downtown to look up a friend of Gwen's, who used to go to her house when she was in Canada. We had dinner there, then went to the Botanical Gardens, which are really lovely. The rock-garden is the largest in the world. Of course there were only a few snow-drops and crocii out, but you could see how lovely it was. They have acres of trees and plants from all over the world, and a load of greenhouses. Some of these were for plants of temperate climate and some for tropical. They had palms, ferns, begonias and vines and plants of all kinds, and one green house full of orchids, which were simply lovely.

Gwen went back there for tea, and I went to find the place where Doris had stayed to pick up some wool the lady was going to buy for her, and to get the clothing coupons that were left. Then Gwen met me at the Legion, we had supper, went to a show they were having there, and then went back to the Cameron's, and to bed.

Monday we brought our bags down and got into the hotel. Mac was coming up Sunday and we were supposed to meet him at noon, so we snooped around the stores in the morning, had dinner at the Legion with him, and then went on a conducted tour of Edinburgh Castle from the Victoria League. The woman who took us knew all the history and that made it more interesting. We went down the Royal Mile, which is the street leading up to

---

[27] Letter is typewritten.

the castle, and the old part of Edinburgh. The castle is up on a very high steep rock, and all the city huddled around it, because it was easily defended, and if they ventured out, the cruel English would attack them. We also saw St. Giles Cathedral, very historic and famous; the market cross where all proclamations of national importance are called by the town crier (yes, still); the heart done in cobble stones which is supposed to mark the heart of Midlothian (the county in which Edinburgh is); and the Scottish national law courts. The castle consists of many parts and is very interesting.

With all that walking, we were content to sit in the Legion at night, drink a coke and then go to the hotel to bed.

Tuesday we went on a tour from the Legion of Holyrood Palace. With this we covered the lower end of the Royal Mile and quite a few old and interesting buildings along the way. The Palace had more insides to it, and historic rooms were preserved—tapestries, beds, etc. This was where Mary, Queen of Scots, carried on her scandalous affair after she conked off her husband. On the way back we went through Lady Haig's Poppy Factory, where veterans were making all sorts of things for sale. It was interesting to watch them doing work which their disability best suited them for. Of course poppies are the main industry, and they have quite a system.

Tuesday night Gwen's friend's sister wanted us to go out to her place, so we corralled Mac and the Merchant Navy boy, hereafter called Billy, into going. We had quite a nice evening, sitting by the fire and chewing the rag about world travels, religion and politics. It came out here that Billy the Kid, who looked about 17, was really 20 and had been in the M.N. for 6 years, and had been in most spots of the world you can think of. He comes from Vancouver. We came home, and after trying to get the boys into the hotel lounge for some tea, and getting told they couldn't come in, they went home and we went to bed.

Wednesday we got up and got a train to Aberdeen. It took 3½ hours, but the country was lovely. Aberdeen looks very clean, because the houses are nearly all made of granite. The most famous building is Marishall College, which is made of granite, with clean straight lines, with gargoyles at the top. It looks very majestic and aloof, but has stayed clean, although it is old. We took a tram out to Aberdeen Beach, which naturally is on the North Sea, and is a wide long beach. As the sun was shining and it was not cold, we walked up and down the beach picking up shells as happy as two kids. We went back to town, had supper and got the 6 o'clock train back to Edinburgh. It was the Perth–London train and was crowded.

Thursday we slept in for a change, just getting up in time for lunch before the 1 o'clock train to Glasgow. After arriving there we looked over the stores. Each bought a Fair Isle beret—which to you is Shetland wool, made in a certain pattern which is called Fair Isle. We met Peggy Walls at 5 o'clock, and she took us home. There was Mary, a teacher, and a married younger brother called, for some mysterious reason, "Wims." We had a lovely supper, had a while to chat before leaving to catch the 9 o'clock train back. A schoolteacher friend of Mary's had made a cake and some cookies for the Canadian girls, and Peggy had even made some candy. I must say that they must have expected royalty. We got back about 10:30, and so to bed.

Friday we did a few odds and ends of shopping, and then with Mac went to Dunfermline. This is very complicated business. First we took a bus down to the bridge—the famous Firth of Forth Bridge. Then we got on a ferry boat to cross, giving us a good look at the Bridge. On the other side we walked about a quarter of a mile, then got another bus to the city of Dunfermline. It is a very old place, the former capital of Scotland before they became civilized. There is the ruins of an old abbey and palace there, and the church standing is also very old, having been restored. There are beautiful big gardens (donated by Andrew Carnegie) along the historic glen. The town is on a hill, or hills, and it seemed we were climbing up and down all day. The deeper into Scotland you go, the more Scotch the people are, and that is progressively good. They are a grand lot.

Friday night there was a dance at the Legion, and while Mac and Gwen went to the dance, I sat by the fire and was lazy. However, don't think that laziness doesn't pay, because the cutest soldier came up and talked to me. Then Mac and Gwen came back and we all sat and gabbed. Finally it got to be 10 o'clock and they kicked us out. We walked to the hotel, dropped our bundles, plus one lemon that Mac had presented me with, then went for a walk through a part of the city that none of us recognized, and probably couldn't find again. We said we'd meet Mac and Bruce (the soldier) the next day, and finally got to bed. Jim and Mabel (from the house) were supposed to arrive Saturday morning, but Jim was sick, so Saturday afternoon matinee was spent with the usual numbers of kids. It also was an old show, but we enjoyed ourselves immensely. Bruce had to go out Saturday night with a friend of his. Mac wanted us to go dancing, but we felt awfully lazy, so just he and Mabel went. While sitting at the Legion, a guy comes up to me and says, "Hello Edna." That isn't very unusual to say, but I couldn't place the guy from Adam. After looking at him blankly, he says, "You met me in London." That was a laugh—and not very distinguishing. However at last I finally placed him as a guy I met at the Legion in London on Thanksgiving with a gang of kids, and went to a show with. He still had to tell me his name, though, it being Hank. Well, Hank had a friend named Joe, and asked Gwen and I to the Palais, which is Edinburgh's leading dance-hall, so we went. It is a super place. They have two orchestras on a revolving stage, one orchestra at a time being out. The floor was good, and we had a very nice mild time. They walked us home, and while we were standing talking at the hotel door the night porter came out to put up the iron gate in front of the door, which seems to be standard equipment all over the U.K. after 11:30 at night. We helped him to put it up and get rid of a drunken sailor, then got to bed.

We got up at 8 o'clock—a Sunday morning, too—to have breakfast, get some sandwiches, check out of the hotel, and get to the station to meet Mac shortly after 10. The trip down was very crowded from Newcastle on—we were lucky to get seats, since this train started from Edinburgh. Of course, there are no diners on trains, and we were on from about 10:30 to 8:30 at night. We had sandwiches, and Mac had got some cokes from the Legion. When we arrived home we were tired and dirty, and by the time I had a bath and put my hair up was ready for bed. I slept like a log for a change—it was simply the change of air. In Scotland I needed very little sleep, but as soon as I arrived back I could feel the heaviness of the atmosphere. Back at work today and, needless to say, finding it hard to settle down.

After having very sparse mail, was pleased to find three letters from Mom, two letters from Blanche and a valentine, valentine and letter from Marg, and a letter from a Mrs. Newman in Toronto with whom I am conducting business on behalf of Mrs. Roe.

If it weren't for Canada, Scotland would be my country. They will tell you it is very poor, and perhaps it is. Maybe that is what makes the people so friendly. The country is pretty, lots of hills, and lots of coastlines. Of course we didn't see the real highlands. I bought a kilt—yes, a real one. It has to be made to measure—apparently it is unthinkable to get a kilt any other way, because you simply just can't go and buy one. The old boy in the tailors was very talkative. He asked me what clan I belonged to. Having consulted a chart beforehand, I told him if I were Scottish it would be the Gunn clan. Whereupon he proceeded to relate all the bloody history of the Gunns for centuries back. Just think—if we had been Scotch we sure would have been fightin' hill-billies. I chose a nice tartan, even if there wasn't much choice, in very good cloth, and I am anxious to see the result. It will be two months, though.

The first thing we were greeted with was the news that repats have been frozen until April—there are lots ahead of me, so you'd better start looking for a hired girl. Oh, well, they say Spring is very nice here, and the summer would <u>have</u> to be better than last summer.

There were a lot of boys from the B.L.A.[28] on leave in Edinburgh—Bruce was one of them, and they sure have some stories to tell. Makes you realize that there really is a war on. They get 7 days clear and sure appreciate it. They really made our mouths water though. It seems they have a huge hamburger stand in Nijmegan—real hamburgers and hot-dogs and Canadian coffee. We made them feel how lucky they were—aren't we hypocrites? Anyway, you can't get anything like that in U.K. Some ice-cream is around in the restaurants, though, and I think conditions are much better around than when we came.

[28] British Liberation Army

Had a letter from Jack (Woods) telling about the glamours of the African sweaterless sweater-girls.

Oh, there was a parcel waiting for me, saying it was from Dorothy in Dad's writing. It was in good condition. We enjoyed the short-bread for tea. Will preserve the toilet paper stuffing. All the letters I got were dated January except the air mail from Mom. By the way, don't you think it might be an idea to date the parcels? Everybody in the office when they get a parcel tears their hair and moans, "Why don't they put a date on it?"

Think I must sign off. Gwen is still writing her letter, has only got to Tuesday afternoon and has written two and a half pages, but I've covered the most important doings. Sorry I didn't write last week but you can see that I was very busy, and I think I have already outdone myself. Will write next weekend, since I am staying home.

Love,
Teddy.

March 5.

Dear Mom & Dad:

Haven't had a particularly eventful week. Was getting over my leave, I guess—saving money (or rather, was broke) and catching up on odd work. Mrs. MacLean took out the extra bed, so Art and I spent an evening re-arranging the furniture. We moved every piece. I have loads of room now, and it will soon be warm enough to have the doors open. Crocuses are up in the park, and there is some kind of a tree with pink flowers out around town. Also bay-buds are green. With the approach of spring we are also heralding the return of fly-bombs, as I suppose you saw in the paper. Even had some German aeroplanes over—the first since last June. However, they bother people as little as they ever did. We had two alerts this morning.

Bert Wilson was in over the weekend. We didn't do much. Stayed home, ate and gabbed, went to a show Sunday. He usually has a polishing streak and shines everything in sight, so my buttons and shoes get cleaned once every two weeks, at least.

I sent Dad a picture I had taken in Scotland. Hope you all like it. Tell Dorothy if she wants one I'll send it, but not unless she wants one.

I sent Blanche a bracelet for her birthday. Hope she gets it. Surface mail, Air mail, registered, and parcels going to Canada between Jan. 18 and 23rd were all lost, so suppose my mail for that week won't get to you. However, I think mail has been poor all winter, but guess you know enough by this time not to worry. I haven't had any mail from you or Blanche for a week and a half.

I suppose by the time this gets to the coast, you will have left, and it will probably follow you all over Canada.

Must sign off now and get to work, hoping I get some mail from you soon.

Love,
Teddy.

March 6

Dear Blanche:

Nothing of any importance this week. I haven't had a letter from you or Mom for a week and a half. Got one from Jack Woods and Marie Mindorff (Jarvis) yesterday. Good old Jarvis has closed down. Mom said that Dad had bought a car, but it took a letter from Jack from Africa to tell me what kind. Of course mail is much quicker from there.

Last week I mailed you an account of my leave and a birthday present. Hope you get it in time. Yesterday I got two books from the book club in Toronto mailed Nov. 6.

Doris has gone home—expect she's there by now. All repats. have been frozen now—fine thing, I think. Spring is practically here. We have had some bigger and better fly-bombs—up to now haven't had any for ages. They even managed to sneak across a few German bombers. Propaganda here is so potent that people were just amazed when the alert went. "Wonder what it is?—Of course Germany hasn't got any airplanes."

Bert Wilson was in over the weekend. We didn't do much. He and I and Art (my neighbour) gabbed—went to a show Sunday. Bert and Art started to tear a gramophone apart. After getting it in as many pieces as possible they got disgusted and threw them all back in the case and closed it.

Mr. Saunders is on leave so I am having a happy week devoted to amendments.

Did you get the pictures I sent? Hope they weren't lost. I got my picture taken in kilt and all the trimmings in Scotland, and sent one to Dad. Did I tell you I bought a kilt?

Well, must get to work.

So long for now,
Edna.

March 12.

Dear Mom & Folks:

Received two Air Mails last week, first in two weeks. Hope you have received some mail from me by this time. Mail is very poor.

Excuse me putting this first, but I don't want to forget it—do you think you could find me a decent hair-brush? Prophylactic, preferably, with good stiff bristles? I'm getting scads of dandruff. Also, I would appreciate some Noxema cream.

Heaven knows when and if you get this, since I don't know where you are about now, think I'll send it to Dorothy. Even if you've left the Coast, don't suppose you'll be at the farm.

Hope you're better by now, Dorothy. Take it easy. I got quite a kick out of Dad having to buy another car. Of all the nerve! I thought about it last night when I walked all the way to the station at Cambridge. I went up there for the weekend. Had a nice quiet time. Went Sat. afternoon and returned last night. The Roes are going to Brighton for Easter holidays and want me to go down. I might, since it isn't long enough to go to Cornwall. It is long enough to go to Liverpool, but somehow I think it would be rather a bleak journey. I'll be near there when (and if) I go home, anyway. No movement yet, but a spiritualist told Kath the European war would be over April 23rd, so we have all made plans to fit.

Blanche writes such pathetic letters about rationing in Washington that I almost feel sorry for her.

Two girls from our Directorate went to the Scilly Isles on leave (off S.W. coast). Between being sea-sick, queer people, and subs chasing around, they just stayed one day and came back to Cornwall to wallow in eggs for breakfast. The food situation is better everywhere than London.

I haven't got your letters here to answer, so I haven't much to say.

Think I had better get back to work. Must sit down and write a decent letter when ordinary mail gets better.[29] For now, anyway, so long.

Love,
Teddy.

March 13

Dear Blanche:

After not hearing from you for some time received 3 letters this week. Sorry you haven't been getting my mail, but guess the crossing is bad both ways.

I haven't been doing much of note since my leave. Went to Cambridge this weekend. Had a nice visit. Went to the Arts Theatre Sat. night and saw "Scandal at Barchester," which was very good. Came back on early train Sunday night. The weather has been quite nice. The Winco arrived back from Canada today, so we expect things to pop tomorrow. He gives us all a pain. He 'phoned from Prestwick, and Mr. Saunders came out to our office and said, "That was the Winco. He's not in the sea after all." We expected him yesterday. We all said, "Too bad." We thought maybe he had heard about last week's rockets and decided to stay away. The instinct of self-preservation is very strong in him.

---

[29] This is written on light-weight blue paper, with the declaration "Armed Forces Air Letter." The paper can be folded and sealed to form its own envelope.

. . .

[Your] Letter of Feb. 27

I had an air mail from Mom which said your dental appointment laid you out. Why don't you get false teeth? I had my teeth checked last week—still O.K. although they tend to go faster over here.

. . .

I haven't been to church since I was at Canterbury. Haven't found one yet. The one just up the street is very high.

If you don't mind, I'll stick to painting. I have learned to cook considerably here, in pure self-defence, so will be tired of it. One meal a day will do me nicely. At that rate will paint the cottage in a week—what will we do the rest of the summer? I think I know what I'll be doing—the same as I am right now—you, too.

There is a form circulating for volunteers for the Allied Control Commission. They are taking girls' names, but not mine, since you are asked to sign for 2 years. If I were 2 years younger I would.

For your information, I can understand the Scottish people better than the English. I had oatmeal for breakfast every morning, but didn't get around to oatcakes or haggis. The two Walls "girls" were riots. Both old maids—one an office fixture, the other a schoolteacher. They were grand to us. Have quite a nice house and are real housekeepers. "Wims," their brother, is younger, and married. He took us down to the station.

Had a nice ride in a car. When we went to Dunfermline the ferry was rather late coming back, and when we were standing shivering waiting for a bus back into Edinburgh a man picked us up and drove us right into town. Right decent of him, eh?

It was funny meeting this chap again whom I went out with once when he was on leave in London last October. He is stationed in the Shetland Isles—a radar mech.

My writing really hasn't deteriorated this much—I'm writing on my knee and the pad isn't stiff.

I thought Dad's farm feet would be getting itchy, so wasn't surprised to hear they have headed back for the farm. Dad wrote me half an Air mail—surprise! and Kenny wrote me a whole Air Mail. Poor Jackson at Tofino! Here's a joke about that dump. F/L Saunders used to work in England. He married an English girl and took her to Canada. He joined the Air Force, got posted to Tofino and took his wife there. Then he got posted to England, couldn't bring her, and there she is, stuck at Tofino, and he's here. He throws such wild parties he's continually getting asked to move.

Was just interrupted by the 'phone—Mr. Robinson, who says he will call me at work to arrange a night to take me out. Says I sound like you—heaven forbid!

Susan Roe is the funniest kid (she is 11 and reads Tolstoy). She went down and stood in line Sat. morning for theatre tickets for Mr. & Mrs. Roe and I. She was beside an old lady of about 80, and for the half hour they stood in the cue [sic] in a deep discussion of Shakespeare. It must have been good. They are going to Brighton for the Easter holidays and want me to go down a day. I don't know if we can travel, but I might go in civvies. I'll see what Bert wants to do.

I have decided the only way to do everything you want to is to have at least two lives. Do you think I'll make a successful career woman? Have I enough brains to get through University? If I thought I'd make a mess of a career I'd get married instead. However, I suppose I can try a career, and then if that fails I can always get married. I don't feel disposed to settle down right now (except when I get fed up), so I suppose I hadn't better. Anyway, it's hard to know.

Last night I couldn't get to sleep, and unconsciously composed a few lines of poetry. I finished it consciously today. Maybe I'm prejudiced, but I think it's good—here is a copy. Remember, copyright's reserved!

Say, there's an idea! I could write for a living. I don't think authors work very hard—that would suit me.

Well, must sign off now—take a bath and get to bed. First I have to find three pennies to work the geyser—God bless England!

As the saying goes—Cheerio—

Love

Edna.

P.S. On hearing the story a second time I don't think they are taking girls for the Control Commission. Thought it sounded a bit fantastic, since they won't even let us go to the continent.

March 20

Dear Blanche:

Haven't heard from you since I wrote last week. Didn't do a lot this week. Wednesday night was our last Philosophy Class. Dr. Lewis called it a "Steeplechase through philosophy," and it sure was. We covered the history of philosophy and main precepts from the Greeks to Bertrand Russel. When I got home Baldy McLean was waiting for me—poor boy! We had a visit and he left fairly early.

Friday night was our Headquarters dance. Five of us from the house went. It was quite good, but could have been livelier. When we came we went to Julia's room for tea, and sat & talked for a while.

Bert was supposed to come in Saturday since he had tickets for the Navy Show, but he got caught in some foul act and got 7 days' kitchen fatigue, so he mailed the tickets. Thoughtful of him—eh? Well, I asked Doug Johnston to go—the corporal in our section. The show was really good. All London is raving about it. They didn't know how good Canadian humour was before. Besides, it has lots of young talent, which is naturally missing from ordinary productions these days. I took Doug home, and the clan gathered for coffee. That's one thing—our gang are not late-night prowlers—transportation may have something to do with it. Coffee was served in the Blue Lounge this time—my room. Doug thinks the gang is wacky, but enjoyed them.

Sunday, Julia and I and Mac and Art started out to meet the B.L.A. leave train. We met Miles, Julia's brother-in-law . . . [pages 3 and 4 missing]

. . . then dial your number. After a long while somebody answers, you answer, they answer again—there the other line is getting angry, "Are you theah?" and there you are shouting, wondering why deaf people answer the 'phone. Then the operator chimes in sweetly, "Press the A-button, please." It's a button on the fore-mentioned box; without pressing this jigger the other end can't hear you. Well, if your number is busy, you press the B button—oh, excuse me, I mean button B—and your money comes back. There is a class of people who make all their money by going around pressing B buttons on pay 'phones and collecting money people forgot to reclaim, or didn't know enough to.

As for a long-distance call, you practically have to have a whole afternoon to spare to make one.

Well, I feel like 'phoning you, but after this, even I feel confused. You'd better ask someone to explain them to you with motions. Really, though, I feel like a veteran and enjoy teaching someone else how to use them.

Well, enough of this "phoney line"—(you can plant that). Must sign off.

Love,
Edna.

March 25.

Dear Blanche:

Received two letters this week—one March 4th, and one March 12th.

Sorry you had such a bad time with your tooth. How do you keep sprouting wisdom teeth? Seems to me you've had a lot of them out. No doubt it was because you were feeling sick that the P.A. sounded so insulting. Anyway, the higher-ups should be told off once in a while—hope I meet the Winco when I'm a civvy.

. . .

I am having a perfectly lazy Sunday. Got up at 1 o'clock, made myself brunch, then just sat and read "A Tree Grows in Brooklyn." I was just doing the dishes when Doug Johnston and his room-mate came. They were just biking by, so dropped in. Probably Doug wanted to show Ted the crazy house. Then little French Bert who used to live here came in, and Morris came down from upstairs, so we had a coffee party. However, they have all gone now.

I got your letters Friday, . . . [and] I got four "Lifes" last week—Dec. 18, 25, 11, and Jan. 22. Mr. Brunker enclosed a note saying that they had been delayed while he moved.

Hope you got your birthday present alright.

Do you like this purple ink? It intrigues me.

I think being away from Canada we get a good perspective on the politics—away from most of the dirt slinging. Here is the real story:—

When McNaughton[30] was in command over here, he didn't get along with Monty,[31] and Ralston[32] toadied to Monty. McNaughton had the first Can. corps perfectly trained, and the backbone of the 1st Div. Ralston took them out and gave them to the British army. Ever since that, McN. has been out for Ralston's hide. At last he gave up the command in protest to Monty's treatment. When he went back, the Can. Army did have enough reinforcements. Ralston judged the condition from numerical reports. These numbers included old crocks held at the units but not really fit for the front line, men waiting for repat, and even the staff of the units.

In June, a man named Connie Smythe, 2nd i/c of an ack-ack battery in France, was wounded and returned to Canada. He gave the Press the story of the real condition of the Canadian soldiers who were being sent into the line. You heard it—untrained, unequipped, and kids. It was true, but unauthorized. It raised a smell, and Ralston came over to investigate. He got booed in every Army camp over here and went back with changed ideas. King & McN. still thought reinforcements were sufficient & Ralston resigned. After McN. got driving, he changed colors and started sending over the Zombies. The English think McN. is a cad, but the troops are starting to see his view-point. As for King, you only have to mention his name for the troops to start holding their noses. There isn't much choice for an election, of course. There is rumour that King will use separation from the Empire as his platform and, if he does, he'll get the service vote. Personally, I don't think he's got enough guts.

The news over the weekend has made me feel hopeful, the first time I have since the invasion, in spite of the optimism that's been rife here all winter.

I went to a pantomime this week. It is strictly an English product, so decided I had better see one. It was "Goody Two Shoes." It has a fairy story running through it, but totally unconnected turns keep popping up all through it. It is more like a variety show. I enjoyed it—the talent was very good.

Bert Wilson didn't get in last weekend, his regular one, so said he was coming this weekend "unofficially," which means without a pass. He hasn't

---

[30] General A.G.L. McNaughton, commander of the Canadian forces in Europe.
[31] Field Marshal Bernard Montgomery, commander of the Allied ground forces at Normandy. He later accepted the German surrender on May 7, 1945.
[32] J.L. Ralston, Canadian minister of defence.

turned up, and hasn't phoned. If he didn't get away from camp he would have 'phoned, so we figure he got picked up at the station here, since the MPs[33] have really turned the heat on all railway stations since those 70 Germans escaped. The country was quite perturbed that so many could get away and stay out so long. I hope Bert didn't get picked up, because he just finished 7 days' kitchen fatigue and won't get off so easy this time. All this crap makes me sick—you'd think we were a bunch of morons. Of course you are assumed to be one unless you kick like hell to get your hooks, then you are credited with half a brain.

Did you know that the way they measure the troops' morale is to read their mail? I saw one dilly written by a kid up North, which had come to the head censor (in our directorate). I wish I knew they'd open one of mine—I'd give them a blast.

We don't know yet if we're getting any extra time off at Easter, but have been told we <u>can't</u> travel. I think that's hell—all the other troops stationed in London and the RCAF in the country get 28 days' leave a year, and we just get 14, then we can't travel at Christmas or Easter.

I do get browned off once in a while, but not nearly as often as I did in Canada. They are playing "Yes, We Have No Bananas" on the radio. Isn't that ironical?

We had a letter from Doris. She didn't get discharged, but got 20 days' leave, then goes into the hospital to get her arm straightened. She said they really gave them a rousing welcome, both at Lachine and at Toronto. I don't think it will be long now for the rest of us.

Julia's husband is here on leave. He has been in Italy. She hasn't seen him for nearly five years.

Guess I had better sign off and get myself something to eat. I am on a 48, but got up early yesterday morning and went to the butchers', thereby getting pork chops. Some luxury! If I ever eat mutton in Canada you can put me away. So long for now,

Love,

Edna.

Because of the great numbers of people who would be travelling over holidays, armed forces personnel were often denied permission to travel at these times. There just wasn't room for us on the trains along with all the civilians.

Historical Notes: By the spring of 1945, the Canadian troops that had done so much to liberate Italy were exhausted and depleted, both in terms of numbers and equipment. However, there were no reinforcements or new supplies to be had, even when the Canadian troops were ordered to northwest Europe to effect the liberation

---

[33] Military police.

of Holland. Needless to say, Prime Minister Mackenzie King, General A.G.L. McNaughton, and Minister of Defence J.L. Ralston did not rate highly amongst the troops.

On the night of March 10–11, 1945, seventy German prisoners tunnelled forty feet to freedom from Camp 198 in Bridgend, South Wales. It was the biggest attempt to escape made by German POWs in Great Britain during the Second World War. All were eventually recaptured.

April 1.

Dear Mom & Dad:

Well, another uneventful week. The last letter I had from you was an Air Mail of March 14th, but I think I had that when I wrote last week.

Got a parcel Thursday, and also one from Blanche. Thanks very much—I'm glad you managed to get a nail brush. Also for the candy and gum—especially gum.

Before I forget to tell you, I sent you some flowers for Mother's Day, so you had better meet the train for about the week before, or ask the station agent to 'phone you if they come. It won't hurt somebody to make a trip for them, since I want you to get them while they're nice.

I had Good Friday, yesterday and today off, but since we couldn't travel I have stayed home, of necessity.

Thursday night I washed my hair and left it straight Friday for a rest. Archie wanted to know why I didn't leave it straight all the time, Mrs. McLean said I looked 18, but other people just looked and shuddered, so I did it up Friday night. I did my washing and ironed on Friday, then at night Mac and Mabel and I went out to a pub across the river at Hammersmith. Saturday I slept in, did my shopping about noon (got some steak that is probably as tough as leather). Then Mabel and I went to meet Julia when she came out of work, we had dinner then went to a show—"The Sign of the Cross." It is an old one with a modern prologue added. We hadn't seen it before, though, and enjoyed it.

Mabel came home, since she had to go to confession, but Julia and I, having nothing to confess, went to a restaurant for supper. We went to the Quality Inn on Leicester Square—about the best restaurant in town—food is better than the expensive places. Of course we stood in line, but the buskers were out entertaining, going from cue to cue [sic] on Piccadilly and Leicester Square. After supper we came home and spent a quiet evening.

This morning we got up, and Julia and I went to a Presbyterian Church. It was quite nice—the service wasn't very long since there was communion after—Julia stayed and I came home. I changed my clothes, cleaned up the room, had coffee and toast. Three of the boys were just in for a chat but have gone now. It is a miserable day for Easter—just like an April day at home, almost. I bet the prairies would look bleak to me, too—we've already had a couple of weeks of spring.

Blanche sent me the cutest candle—made like a fat rabbit sitting on his haunches—it is yellow, so I have it sitting beside a pitcher of daffodils and it looks charming.

Bert didn't get in this weekend because of the travel ban, but will be in next week. He 'phoned Tuesday night, and I was out, but he called later, and he 'phoned Friday night when I was out—the only two nights all week I was out.

I saw "Peer Gynt" Tuesday night. It was very good—a psychological play. The actor was good, and it was staged well.

The war looks good, so maybe I will be home before Fall.

There really is nothing more to say, so I better sign off. Hope to get some mail this week. Look after yourselves.

Love,
Teddy.

I saw Laurence Olivier and Ralph Richardson star in this production of Peer Gynt.

April 7/45.

Dear Fat:

I note this is your birthday—I hope you had a nice time. Did someone make you a cake? Hope you got the present I sent—it was registered.

Got your letter of March 19th yesterday. Baltimore sounds nice—but I always connected it with the deep South. Just hark your memory back to those "absolutely straight up and down" houses and that is Holland Road to a T. The steps go right up practically off the street. We have an innovation here that I'll bet Baltimore hasn't got—beside the steps is a set of steps going down to the sub-basement. Usually there is another family living in that part of the house. In the days of affluence, before they were all turned into rooming houses, that is where the servants lived. In our house, where Mrs. McLean, Art and I live, the scullery is at the front, under the road.

Speaking of bananas, it was in the paper that England is starting to get bananas in, but haven't seen any yet. Things are really getting quite good here. You can get ice-cream now. True, it is the English idea of ice-cream but, nevertheless, goes very good. People are eating more of it now than they ever did, just because they have been so long without it and, of course, the Americans and Canadians have built up quite a market for it.

So far, April hasn't been as nice as March was. We have started parades in the morning again, and this morning I was quite chilly. The rockets are over (the papers say).

I agree with you—the nicest things are the wools. The tartans and Shetland Wool we saw in Scotland were simply lovely. I bough a Fair Isle beret (Shetland Wool) and a square woollen scarf with paisley design on it, although it is not real paisley. The silver in England is beautiful, too, but a terrible price. There is about a 200% tax on it. I saw a pair of small plain beautiful George II pitchers yesterday for about £12. You can't buy painted china in England—it is all exported.

I saw the Student Prince last summer here, and it was a very poor performance—the prima donna sang through her teeth. And, to make it worse, I blundered into another light opera she was singing in before I knew it was her.

Yes, indeed, I saw the inside of the War Memorial. It is the newest part that has been built on the castle. It really is beautiful—you can believe your Scotchmen. It is all marble inside and the windows are arranged so that the lighting is super. There is a niche for every Scottish regiment. It was built around the highest point in the castle, and they just left the rock jutting through the floor. There is also a niche for Canadian Scottish regiments.

Also went into the oldest part of the castle, which is St. Margaret's chapel. It is very tiny—just about room for 6 people, and very sweet.

I didn't write my account in very much detail, but it is hard to think of it all at once. The pictures I took all turned out, and I will send them with this letter. You can send them on to the rest of the family. I sure learned a heck of a lot of history—I think I could get quite interested in English history now, and before I simply loathed it. You know how Mom wanted to name me after both her and Dad and couldn't find one name to do both? Well there was a Saxon queen named Ediva and I am going to change my name to that, and give Myrtle the air.

I am writing this at the office. I have work to do, but it seems the harder you work, the less thanks you get. I have the monthly Diary to type out, but it isn't due until the 10th, and I don't see why I should spoil them by having it in ahead of time. Monday will be soon enough.

I haven't been doing much this week. I have felt awfully tired, although I have been getting enough sleep—it must be the climate. Spring here isn't bracing like it is at home. Today is misty and fairly cold. Easter Sunday was miserable and rainy, but Monday was lovely.

I made a haul yesterday—I was walking down High Holborn looking for a phonograph parts shop when I met FL/O McEwan (she used to be at Jarvis as an AW2) coming out of a dark dingy shop. She said to me, "Look what I got in there," and furtively showed me a jar of <u>Elizabeth Arden</u> cream. I buzzed right in and got a jar of cleansing cream, and also noted in a dark corner some photographic printing paper, which is very hard to get, so I got some for Rita—whose hobby is photography. We can get a few E.A. cosmetics at the K. of C.[34] on Regent Str., but I seldom go down there. The beauty of those canteens is that they get in shipments of special stuff from Canada, and will only sell it to Canadians. The trouble at home is that [people regard] all those

---

[34] Knights of Columbus

organizations as only some obscure thing that they have to donate to every once in a while, but I don't know what we'd do without them. The Canadian Legion is the best, then the Salvation Army, then the K. of C. The Y.M.C.A. is nothing extra—they are all out in the field and contain a lot of profiteers.

Papers are just full of plans for V-Day—most of them quite advanced. Everybody is quite convinced that there never will be a time when the Germans stop fighting and there is a definite time we can say the war is over. V-Day will simply be a proclamation that the war is considered over, and fighting will go on all the time until the complete reorganization plans for Europe are carried out.

Well, must sign off—sorry there is so little news. Hope I don't forget to enclose the snaps.

Love
Edna.

April 11.

Dear Blanche:

I must be getting feeble-minded or something because I can't remember whether I thanked you for the Easter parcel and it has been bothering me all day. If I haven't, sorry I forgot so long, but if I have, twice won't hurt any.

We enjoyed the fudge—glad you can cook something. Everything had a delightful layer of pink clover powder, but it only perfumed it wonderfully. I think I salvaged most of the powder, and it is very nice. We all fell in love with the bunny—I christened him Joey. He went nicely with my Easter daffodils. He now guards a jar of narcissus, but they are almost out of season, too, and tulips are coming in. I'll see if I can get yellow or mauve ones, because he'll certainly clash with red.

Today I was moved to the D.A.S.'s office—a G/C.[35] There is a corporal and I in his outer office. He has an office of his own—with a rug. We just got a new one (G/C, not rug) and he seems much more human than the former one. Although it is a complete change of work, it is in the same directorate, so I know all the kids.

I got my teeth cleaned today and they feel funny. Still in perfect condition. I certainly know better than to grow wisdom teeth, and I bet you're been cured of growing them.

Bert was in last weekend and expects to be in this weekend also.

I sent you an ordinary letter[36] with some snaps last weekend. Will write again this weekend. So long for now—I am trying to get to bed by 9:30.

Love
Edna.

---

[35] Group Captain
[36] This is an air mail letter.

April 10/45.

Dear Mom & Dad:

Got your Air mail of March 21st last Monday. Haven't done much all week. Bert came in Saturday. He and Mac and I went to the dog races—just in time to see the last two races. We stopped off for supper at Bertorelli's. We then came back home and went out to the pub. Came home about 10, and I made coffee. The gang drifted home one by one as usual. When Mabel came home she happened to remark it was a nice night, so she and Mac and Bert and I went out for a walk about 1 o'clock. We passed two red lanterns on a pile of bricks. Two seemed unnecessary, so we blew one out and it was carried home under one of the boys' arms. What to do with it?—it is ugly and red and square with a red lens on two sides—burns oil, I guess. Well, it is going to be enamelled white and hung in my room. It will be quite picturesque. I always had a secret yen for a street light, but this will do. Sunday we loafed around, but at last the nice day got us out, and we went for a long walk. When we came home I cooked dinner—quite a change for me, but it was good. Bert thinks I can cook now.

Got a parcel from Aunt Maude this week. Also one from you folks but, again, no date on it. Thanks a lot—it's all the little luxuries we get from home that make life bearable. This parcel had rice krispie cookies, coffee, lump sugar, milk, tomato juice, bars, gum and Prem.[37] Do you remember when it was sent? Aunt Maude must have spent ages collecting hers—there was a box of chocolate, cooking chocolate, tin of peanuts, honey, toothbrush, tooth powder, bars, gum, etc. I must write her right away.

I have enough money to get along. I am going on leave again in May or June but don't think I'll need any more. I have saved some and might as well spend it since it is hard to get it home. I subscribed to another bond. If I have $80 you couldn't have taken much money out. You should keep some out—in case you would ever want some money and you can't get it out of my account. What about my coat storage bill? Here's hoping I'm wearing it next winter. If I got home now I'd have to do a lot of talking to get my discharge.

I started a new job today—but it is a different section within the Directorate so it isn't like a complete change, since I know all the kids. I am in the Orderly Room. The new officers are nice and the work will be interesting.

Well, must sign off and get to bed—no matter how much sleep I get here I still hate getting up.

Take care of yourselves—
Love,
Teddy.

---

[37] Canned meat.

April 14/45.

Dear Mom & Dad:

Received your Air Mail of March 29 this week. I almost reeled with surprise, of course, to discover Dad had written so much. I was very pleased to hear from him. I refrained from comments before, but I think the picture is pretty super—the gang all said I handled that sword as if I had used one all my life. No, mother dear, I did not buy a whole outfit. The kilt alone took 15 coupons, and I'm afraid to tell you how much money. However, I hope to get the whole outfit eventually—I imagine I will be able to get it in Canada. I almost died when I priced sporrans, and I want a nice one. The material I picked was beautiful—hard—I'll bet the pleats will be like knives. I couldn't afford hand-woven, but this is very close to it. By the way I haven't got the kilt yet, but expect it any day now.

Imagine having that much snow the last of March! I had a letter from Marg saying they also had a lot in Calgary. It was real warm here then, and it is hard to imagine snow. I'm afraid I'll have to get acclimatized all over again. . . .

I suppose you were right at home with the chicks in the kitchen—you could wash their feet twice a day instead of just at night. However, I hope they grow up into good layers and eaters. The man at the store told me yesterday we should soon look like eggs because we've had so many—7 in the last six weeks!

I haven't seen Baldy for a few weeks—he works nights a lot. Nicky isn't married yet—she was going to to get married last June, but Winnie had to have the invasion then, and she has been waiting for the man, whoever he is, to come back on leave. At least I saw her three weeks ago and she wasn't married then.

I haven't heard from Elmer or Barney for quite a while—I imagine they are both in Germany—most of the Canadians are. We have a Canadian squadron operating from a field in Germany—or did you see that in the paper?

No, I don't remember Uncle Bert Patterson—he must have been just one of the hundred odd who insisted I come to see them sometime.

Of course, London is all upset about Roosevelt. The Court is in mourning, whatever that means.

Marg said she received an Air mail from me in 5 days—the quickest she had ever got one.

This week has been lovely—I hope it keeps up over the weekend. Bert is coming in this afternoon.

. . .

Did I tell you that we have parades in the morning now? It is really nice out in the mornings, but we have to get up much too early—usually a little before 7, and Mabel and I usually have to run for the bus. We always dash to the corner, hoping to hop one at the light, but that seldom happens the mornings we really want to hurry. We have to walk a block down the street to the bus stop.

. . .

Well this is all. I'm going to ask the Major for an additional officer to work for, since there really isn't enough here for two.

Love,
Teddy.

April 17/45.

Dear Blanche:

Sorry to be late writing this week, but you know how it is. Received your letter last week of March 26.

Got left alone Saturday morning, because Fran was on a 48. Not only was our new Groupie in, but the ex-Groupie arrived also. However, they are both away now, and the acting DAS has gone out. There really isn't enough here to keep us both busy, and I'm wondering who's going to go nuts first—but I think it's going to be me. Even if you have nothing to do, you can't sit and write letters. . . .

It's summer here. The weather is as warm as June at home. Trees are out in full leaf.

You can't possibly have neuritis—only old ladies in wheelchairs get that. . . .

I discovered all my shoes are like yours—all with holes—and Bert bawled me out, so I am starting to get them repaired. They sure do a messy job, but I guess you take it and be thankful you are walking on leather.

Didn't do much through the week—washed my hair, did my laundry, went to one show (Guest in the House). Bert came in Saturday afternoon, and a gang of 10 of us went to a show Sat. night. It was "Hangover Square" and I expected it to be better than it was. We had coffee in Mabel's room. Julia is leaving for home right away, so her brother-in-law Miles was in over the weekend, together with a girlfriend that we didn't even know he had. She is quite nice, and didn't think us too crazy. Well, we got to bed reasonably early—12:30. Sunday morning, Julia and Bert and I got up and went to Church (Presbyterian). My system could hardly stand the shock. Sunday afternoon 10 of us (not the same 10), but the same basic gang, went to Kew Gardens. It was lovely out there, and the day was warm. There are acres and acres, and it is well-kept. There are dozens of varieties of trees and flowers. A lot of the trees were in flower. In spite of the poem:

"Go down to Kew in lilac time,
In lilac time, in lilac time,
Go down to Kew in lilac time
It isn't far from London"

The gang in Kew Gardens, April 1945.

—with all the stress on lilacs, we only saw one lilac tree in flower, but it was lovely. By the way I can't remember who wrote that, but we studied it in school, and I thought he was a silly ass.[38] We left about 6 o'clock. Some of the kids went to a show, I cooked supper. I can cook, no lie, in fact I even eat it. Bert had to leave about 9:30, then I shone my buttons, put up my hair and got to bed. Last night I was supposed to go out to ball practice, but I was too tired when I got home to go out again. I had been duty clerk, even though I didn't do anything but pull the curtains. They moved the offices around yesterday, and now, just when I was learning where people were, they have all moved, and I have to go through that again.

Last week I took two aptitude tests at Personnel Counselling—one like we had on enlistment, and a clerical aptitude test. They just turned out average—I didn't expect any better. Anyway, S/O Bott is going to line up all the occupations that tie up with them this week. She is going to have me in business. Either a small shot in a big firm, or a big shot in a small firm. Personally, I think teaching is less trouble, because people don't expect teachers to be brilliant. She thought my Air Force experience would be good, but I assured her very quickly that the Air Force had not helped me at all. I think I would have learned more about business procedure and administration if I had been with a company for three years than I have in the Air Force in three years. Wouldn't this typewriter frost you? It is just new and has cork paper holders on the paper-holding rod instead of rubber.[39]

Bert and I celebrate our three years' service at the same time—next Tuesday. He starts leave on Monday night, is coming in then, spending Tuesday here, and going up North to visit his cousin, coming back Friday, and Mabel and Mac and Bert and I are going to Brighton. I haven't been there yet, and apparently one must see Brighton.

---

[38] "The Barrel Organ," by Alfred Noyes (1880–1958).
[39] The quality of type on this letter is very poor.

Sunday afternoon, you should have seen us trying to get Archie on the bus. Nearly everybody was down at the bus stop, Bert was standing in the hall keeping Archie moving, and Mac and I were standing out on the side-walk hollering, and keeping an eye to see if a bus was coming. Well, one appeared around the corner just as Archie was putting on his tie. We stayed coaching, and we three had to run and just got it. It was pulling away, when Archie came flying out the door, coat and hat in hand. He ran like mad for about half a block, but gave it up, and piled his clothes on the top of a post (not a pole, a square cement fence post—the good old solid English kind) and finished dressing in the street. We waited at Shepherd's Bush for him, and he came on the next bus. We all lined up on the street and cheered for him when he arrived. Good old Archie—never a dull moment.

I just answered the phone, and it was Group Captain McNabb—none other than your friend Ernie, who used to take the tops off the trees at Sask. Campus. By the way, is Archie McN. still Lieutenant Governor of Saskatchewan, or have the C.C.F.'s closed up Government House? . . .

I got a book from Personnel Counselling called "The Art of Being a Successful Business Girl." It is American and well-written, with good cartoons, even if it doesn't have a great deal more in it than we learned in Business College, or common horse sense.

Well, sorry I can't rake up more news. I will write next weekend, since I am going to have a nice quiet time (except for a D.A.S. party) and no company.

Love,
Edna.
Encls:
Canterbury pictures.

April 23/45.

Dear Blanche:

Everything has been very quiet this week, so not much to report. Didn't get a letter from you last week.

Julia left for R Depot this week, and we had a "do" for her on Tuesday night. We had a lot of fun, and just about tore down the house with noise. Thursday night we had a ball practice for our DAS team which took the shape of playing a game against the DAS men. We had a lot of fun. It was my first time out and, needless to say, I was stiff the rest of the week. Saturday afternoon Mabel and I went to see "Yellow Sands" with Cedric Hardwicke. He is good, and the whole play was very enjoyable. Sunday I was just lazy, did odd jobs, and didn't even dress. Everybody else went out, and I didn't have any company. I was conserving my strength for this week.

Friday I got six more "Lifes" dated between Jan. 29 and March 12. They are delivered to the house. Somebody brings them up and asks if Miss

Mabel MacRae

Johnson is in and always leaves them. I asked Mrs. MacLean to describe him, but she wasn't very definite—just said he wasn't very old and came at noon hour—that wasn't very much help. I borrowed a 120 camera so I could take some pictures at Brighton this weekend.

Tonight the W.D.[40] ball league starts. We are playing C.R., who have had a lot of practice. Also one of our girls hasn't turned up this morning—hope she floats in before night. The Deputy A.O.C.[41] is throwing in the first ball. If he looks any good guess we'll grab him, since our pitcher is a little out of trim. I expect we'll get our slacks trimmed off us, but we'll have fun. We are playing in Hyde Park, near Marble Arch, so should collect quite a crowd. There are always a gang of Americans around there. Not that it takes a ball game to collect Americans.

Bert is coming in tonight, staying tomorrow, and going up North Wednesday. Reimer is coming in Wednesday, so I hope to see him this time. Bert is coming back Friday night and then Mac and Mabel and he and I are going to Brighton. I will send you some pictures of this super-summer-resort. They call it London by the Sea—as if London wasn't close to the sea. If Limehouse wasn't in the way we'd have gulls nesting on our window sills. I'm afraid I won't get to see Limehouse—the police go around in 4's there.[42]

I haven't done hardly a thing since I came down to the DAS. Shortly after I came, the G.C. went on a trip, and when he came back he got posted and whizzed out of here like a streak of lightning. So far we haven't got anybody. The chap who usually comes and sits in his chair is also posted, and our replacement hasn't arrived yet. I am getting callouses, and not on my feet.

---

[40] Women's Division
[41] Air Officer Commanding
[42] Part of the docklands and home to a large Chinese community, Limehouse had a poor reputation. Plus, it was badly bombed during the war.

(Time out for tea)

I haven't had any mail at all this week. In fact, there has been little for anybody.

Well, how do you like that? Our ball game has just been cancelled because the Army want the diamond. Of all the nerve! I think we ought to have a practice anyway, since everybody has their slacks here, and naturally have no plans for the night, expecting the game. Except me—but Bert can always wait. Poor Bert—he has the patience of Job, just like Vic had. By the way, do you remember Vic Racher, who sold his farm so he could join the Air Force, and painted the wood-work of his house yellow, and whose mother was going to teach me to cook? Well, I got Art to check up on his records, to see if he ever made aircrew. He did—A.G.,[43] and was over here until last September, and was re-patted. One of the lucky ones who finished his tour or, of course, he may have been wounded.

I have been over to Personnel Counselling again. By my tests, they want to put me in business, so I chose Private Secretary (naturally with capitals) or junior executive. They recommended an Arts course with Economics and Political Economy. I think it would be better just to take a pass Arts, and maybe take an extra course or two in something Commercial, than struggle with an Honours course. Anyway, I must take time to go to the Education section and look at the Saskatchewan calendar. Too bad B.C. hasn't got a better U. when Mom & Dad are out there during the wintertime. You can cook for me if you want—we get $60.00 per month to live on besides our tuition, and we are allowed to earn up to $40.00 more per month. Besides which I will be getting five cheques of $96.00 each, as well as my $158.00 on discharge. I hope with this I can put off cashing my bonds until I'm finished and really need them. I bought another one, since I have been buying one all the time, and you don't miss what you don't get. Lucky I'm Overseas, or I would have

Edna at bat in Regent's Park

---

[43] Air-gunner

to be paying income tax. Our gratuities are not taxable, cannot be attached, seized or assigned. One thing I'm going to do when I get home is stay in a posh hotel room with towels and soap, and have ham and eggs in bed (as a starter). Well, must sign off. Hope you get the pictures I sent last week.

Lots of Love,
Edna.

May 3/45.

Dear Fat Stuff:

I'll admit I am late getting your letter written this week, but I do write you every week, except when I'm mad at you. I have received two letters since I last wrote. Bert has been in on leave from a week ago Monday until yesterday. We had a good time, usually with Mabel and Mac. We had a grand time at Brighton, even though it did snow. On our way down Saturday morning we stopped off at Hayward's Heath, because Mac used to be stationed down there. It is a pretty town. We had dinner there, and it snowed. At Brighton we went to a dance, walked along the water-front (where we nearly froze in the snow, sleet, rain, etc.) and went to a hockey game. These games are put on just for entertainment, and most of the players are from the Canadian Army. Turk Broda is goalie, and I think most of the Canadians go just to razz him. Giesbrecht, formerly with Detroit, stood at the boards and spent the whole time riding him. He answered back spiritedly, and it was great fun. We had seats by the boards, and at the end of the second period as Broda went by I hollered, "Never mind, Turk, we still think you're wonderful." He turned to see who his one remaining fan was, but couldn't figure out whether I was kidding or not. We saw a lot of the town. It would be nice in summer. The beach is very long and has two big piers with dance halls, bathing pavilions, etc. on them (now closed). There is a pavement all along, just behind the beach, paddling pool, gardens, etc. Most of the beach has been cleared of mines, but there is still one part wired off. We stayed at a guest house the K.C. had got for us, in Hove, but within walking distance of Brighton proper. I took pictures and hope they turn out.

Yesterday, I thought I'd die. As near as I can figure out I had stomach flue (no, that's something in a chimney—flu then). I couldn't keep anything down, so didn't bother eating. I had a cup of tea for breakfast, and lost that. I had a cup of tea for dinner and tea, and kept those, but had some soup at night and didn't keep that. Bert was going to go back after supper, but took me home after work and got me to bed, and then left. I have had spells like that before, but usually shook them through the day, but I was also sick last night. However, am okay today, although shaky.

It has been released that the Canadians are all out of Italy. That was sure kept under cover—the boys had to take all their badges off in transit, and it took them 9 days. Guess Jerry got a surprise in Belgium. They are all getting

9 days' leave here, gradually—I have talked to quite a few of them.

Well, as you know, we have no more rockets, and most people here seem very optimistic. Plans are rushing ahead for V-day celebrations which, as much as I can gather, is that everything is going to close.

. . .

"A Song to Remember" didn't quite appeal to me, although it has been here quite a while. Last week saw Fred Allen and gang in "The Fifth Chair" it was crazy, and also Carmen Miranda in "Something for the Boys".

The news has sure been breaking this week. I don't see how much could happen at once. My idea is that they have just lifted the ban, or it has just leaked out. Somebody here is always trying to stir up trouble with the Russians in the news. If it isn't one bright M.P. it's a Senator. First it was about the Russians in P.O.W. camps here, then it was about some prominent Poles who are missing. Russia is going to be hard to appease and I'd hate to be fighting against her.

Mom told me they were doing some fixing with some foundation, but I couldn't gather what one. She is terrible for not telling the news.

(Must do some work)

Later

Well, they say V-day won't be this week—doubtless it would spoil our weekend, but early next week. Here's to it. Will write you Monday, since I am going to Portsmouth Sunday.

Love,
Edna.

Historical Note: People from all walks of life signed up to serve their country during World War II, and professional hockey players were no exception. Regarding the players mentioned in these letters, Johnny Bower, eventually one of the game's greatest goalies, lied about his age so that he could enlist in the army. Although he was only fifteen, he was eventually called up by the Queen's Own Cameron Highlanders and shipped to England. In 1943, the Toronto Maple Leafs' Turk Broda, another goalie, joined the army and went off to England for two years, mainly to play hockey. And Conn Smythe, known for building Maple Leaf Gardens and presiding over the Toronto Maple Leafs during their glory days, served as a major in both world wars. These men often continued to play hockey overseas to help raise troop morale, so it wasn't unusual to see many of the game's best players participating in the equivalent of pick-up hockey games.

May 9/45.

Dear Blanche:

Well, this is what we've been waiting for, and what a commotion! It was really something to see cold, mind-my-own-business Londoners prancing around with paper hats or wearing ribbons, carrying flags—some of them even forgot themselves so far as to carry noisemakers, and went whistling or rattling along the Strand. People went around in gangs—singing down the

Trafalgar Square on VE Day, May 8, 1945. Photo Credit: RCAF O/S HQ.

George VI, Queen Elizabeth, and Princess Elizabeth on VE Day, May 8, 1945. Photo Credit: RCAF O/S HQ.

street. They'd throw their arms around other people's shoulders and they'd all join in. I heard the greatest variety of songs—from "Tipperary" to the "Volga Boatman."

Monday night they announced VE day would be Tuesday, but people didn't wait to start celebrating. None of us went to work—we have two days off the same as everybody else—one to celebrate and one to recover. Monday night I stayed home, but I hear Piccadilly and Leicester Square were mobbed. Tuesday we relaxed and didn't do anything of note. About 7 o'clock, Art and I and Mac and Mabel started downtown. Bus after bus passed us. By 7:45 we had got as far as South Kensington. We gave up the idea of going through Piccadilly and went to Charing Cross, and walked down the Strand to Trafalgar Square. There was no traffic—only ambulances—there couldn't have been. This is where the mob was. People were all over the lions and the steps of poor old Nelson's monument. Everybody was pushing and shoving, but the shovees just waved flags in shovers' faces. The U. of London manifested themselves here in a long, noisy impromptu parade. They were decorated with anything that came to hand, it appeared, and waving signs filched from anywhere. The tide was going down the Mall, so we went down. Here is where people were really singing. Gangs arm in arm across the road took everything in their stride. We ended up, with thousands of others, on the steps of Victoria's monument in front of the Palace. What a squash! Imagine a bus that is jammed full so you can't raise an arm, and that was it—only we were there for an hour, and it kept surging so that sometimes you were bent backwards and sometimes forward, but hardly ever on your own feet. Well, we listened to the King's speech on the loudspeakers, then waited while he combed his hair and the Queen put on her hat (20 minutes). Then the family came out on the balcony. Poor Mac! He had to lift Mabel up, and then me. We had lost Art by this time. After they went in, we started to leave. I was simply a wreck and who should I meet but F/O Smith, the former educational officer at Jarvis. We made our way across to Green Park and folded up. Well, then we started to think how dry we were and decided to come home. We walked across Green Park—couldn't even get near that tube station, so we walked on to Hyde Park Corner—there was a cue [sic] a block long just waiting to get into the station. Incidentally, it was a beautiful night, and warm, and dozens of people fainted in the crowd. As we left they turned the floodlights on the Palace. Quite a few buildings were flood-lit, signs were lit up, windows lighted, car lights on—it sure looked odd after a year. There are no street lights on now, but they weren't missed.

Oh, yes, we were at Hyde Park Corner. Well, we took a deep breath and went on to Knightsbridge. A bus came along, and passed—full. That was the last one, but we sat on the curb—I copped the ash can to lean on—and waited hopefully.

(Time out—Art and I just heard a piano so we walked down the court. An American was playing beside an open window, so we shouted in to ask if he would take requests. He did, so we sat outside on the grass and listened to him play. He was as completely unsurprised as if strange women in housecoats hollered to him through the window every day.)

Well, we finally forsook the garbage can at Knightsbridge and plodded on. We got down to Albert Hall. There was a huge bonfire in front of the Albert Memorial across the street. They were also setting off flares. We reached one pub only that was open. All they had was lemonade, but it was wet. Our own High St. looked good. Barker's, a huge department store, was well lit and looked super. The town hall was also flood-lit. We finally made it to Holland Road about 11:30 to discover our own pub was still open. We quickened the pace and popped in. Mac ordered pints with no arguments from us. Well, all the local characters were there. About 6 middle-aged women did a conga up and down the floor. People were singing like mad. French Bert, who used to live here, had a flag draped around him. The place had its usual quota of Canadians. The Howarth family (friends of Mac's) were there. One old boy had a glass of about 2 gallon capacity and made great inroads on it. At closing time, Bert conducted patriotic songs, standing on the bar. Finally we got home and went to Mabel's room for coffee. I stumbled to bed and hardly remember hitting the pillow.

After getting separated from us, Art went back to Trafalgar Square. There were four spiffed sailors bathing in the fountain pool (about 18" deep). Water was oozing all over—out of their boots, etc. One took off his pants. When being persuaded to put them on, he insisted they were wet. Well, they were, but not any wetter than the rest of him. Art then met an officer who had a bottle of whiskey in one pocket and two glasses in the other. They proceeded to walk home, partaking as they came.

I was dead this morning. We're not exactly next-door neighbours of George and Lizzie. It's almost five miles from the Palace to here. I woke up about 10:30 when Mrs. McLean brought in some tea and toast, but the next thing I knew it was five to two.

It's almost worth the year over here to be in London on VE night. Maybe it didn't make thousands of people consoled to their losses but, in spite of it, everybody was happy. It made one feel good to be in uniform.

Since I don't want to have to pay postage on this I'd better sign off. I'll tell you about my trip to Portsmouth last Sunday in my next letter. By the way, did you throw out all your secret files yet, like you were going to do? I expect to work damn hard the rest of the week.

So long for now,
Love
Edna.

P.S. I can't write all this again to Mom & Dad—how about sending it on?

Outside Buckingham Palace on VE Day, May 8, 1945.
Photo Credit: RCAF O/S HQ.

May 17/45.

Dear Blanche:

Received two letters this week after not getting any last. In fact, I hit the jack-pot of mail.

We all liked your snap, but the argument of whether you were standing under some flowers or whether that is a hat caused a major split in our office.

Most of April wasn't as warm as March here, but this last week has been nice. In fact, we all went out in bathing suits and shorts last Saturday afternoon to the court at the back, and almost caused a riot in the neighbourhood. Reimer was in town for a few hours on his return from Ireland, but was with a gang and couldn't make it to see me, although he phoned, and I made him promise to come up his first day off. Thanks for the candy effort—hope you won't have to bother much longer. We used to think of home as something definitely future, but we even think we might make it this summer now. Just when we get dreaming of cakes with 2" thick marshmallow icing at home, what do they do? Cut the sugar ration!

There are sure a lot of R.C.A.F. P.O.W.'s in here all day, and it's sure good to see them. Some of them act just like kids, some take it as a matter of course as if they had just come off leave, and some are just bewildered.

Whether Blanche was standing under some flowers or wearing a hat caused a major split in our office. Washington, April 1945.

I think it was rather nice knowing about the peace ahead of time—gave everybody time to prepare. If you like running into a bunch of Canadian uniforms in a foreign country, you should come to London. When you hit our little colony you see nothing else but, then walk down Chancery Lane a ways and you will run into a mob of Canadian Army types.

. . . All the little evacuees are coming back now, with accents from every other part of the British Isles. . . .

Speaking of pictures, I think I am getting some wonderful color shots of Flying Bombs across our district. Bofors guns[44] make a beautiful color track. So does ordinary flak—although I'll never forget Mac yanking us out of the

---

[44] A type of light anti-aircraft gun with single or twin 40-mm barrels.

street when we stood and gaped at it. Well, we weren't used to combat conditions—we had only been in London a week.

I want to try and get something to bring home to the family from England. I was just at the Old Curiosity Shop and got you a mate for your petit point picture. It is about the same size, but in a gilt frame, and I bet it didn't take that little Victorian gal three years to do hers, besides, it's finer.

Sunday morning we had Church Parade. The fall-in was at 8 o'clock, but I joined the choir on Saturday and didn't have to go until 9. Of course I didn't join just because it gave me more sleep—I wouldn't do that! (Somebody rudely remarked that I certainly worked all the angles—it was my boss.) Anyway, we commandeered St. Giles in the Fields, Holborn District, at the end of Shaftesbury Ave. There were 1400 Protestants and, needless to say, a very long parade. Afterwards we had a march-past the mayor of Holborn (red robes, etc. and I almost hit my nose on the mace that the bearer had stuck out) then further down past our A.O.C. We were really smart there.

Last Friday night one of our Engineering Officers from a squadron and his brother-in-law (captain in the Canadian Grenadier Guards) were in town and wanted F/O Kennedy to get three girls to go out, so we three from the office went. We were a little leery, but went, and had quite a good time. We went to one of these dime-and-dance restaurants. Kennedy insisted on keeping me happy, and though he is such a drip in the office he is a lot of fun. He was a little afraid I might take advantage of it in the office, I think, but I certainly looked him in the eye next morning and went back to our usual cool relationship.

I am still in Engineering. S/L Quinn asks for another week, etc., and next week Doug is on leave and I will have to stay then. The week after that the D.A.S.'s corporal is going on leave and is still planning on me to spell her off, and I haven't even seen the new Groupie, let alone get to know his idiosyncrasies.

This Sunday is Whitsun. I don't know why, but it is a general holiday, and they almost floored us by giving us Saturday, Sunday and Monday off. So, I will write you a decent letter then, and try to get back on my schedule. This social whirl! Tonight I am going home for a change, but I have so much to do that I probably still won't get to bed very early. I was lucky to get an appointment for a permanent Saturday morning. I eventually got tired of doing my hair up every night. I saw Barney Knutson Monday night, but I will tell you about that in my letter.

Don't work too hard—
Love,
Edna.

London Eng.
May 23

Dear Blanche & Mom & Dad:

Received a letter from you today, Fat. I really am surprised. Don't see how the War Dept. is going to hold together—particularly if I leave London soon.

. . . Listen, there isn't going to be any civilian travel until we get home—or if there is it will be mad. We have been just as busy. Nobody has told Air Ministry yet that the war is over, and the stuff still comes rolling in. Besides that we handle maintenance personnel training for 2nd Phase.

You never write but you're describing some new clothes, which means you must buy something new every week. I have forgotten what summer clothes look like. . . .

Your parcel arrived Friday. Thanks as lot, Fat. I already had Kath's 120 camera, so kept it a while longer. Took some snaps at Windsor castle.

I guess I never did tell you about Portsmouth. Well, it was a conducted tour. We gathered at Waterloo station. Mr. Spence did manage to get a carriage (get that—no wonder they call me Limey) reserved for us. It is about 1? hrs. trip. We walked from the station down a street to a pier, then walked along the pier and waterfront for about two miles. The walk has various memorials etc. along it—an anchor from the Victory, and a rock behind which two sailors held off a gang of Cossacks in the Crimean War. We couldn't see how even one sailor got behind it. After getting all this way down we took a bus back to the dockyards. There a typical rotund British C.P.O.[45] met us and took us in, where, unfortunately, we had to leave our cameras. We went all over H.M.S. Victory—pulled up in dry dock and looking pretty perky with fresh paint. We had a guide—couldn't figure out whether he came from Wales or Northumberland. The old boat has 130 cannon—real masterpieces—they are

Edna at Windsor Castle, wearing the kilt she bought in Scotland, May 1945.

---

[45] Chief Petty Officer

on all three decks. A small staff of sailors live on it to keep it in order and they also have some sort of class there. The place where Nelson died has a rope around it, with wreaths all the time. They even have old lanterns below—don't know whether they are original or not. It was all very interesting, but we wanted to see bigger stuff, and so were conducted down to a dock and on to H.M.S. Malaya. It has just been taken out of action and is being turned into a training ship. Part of the old crew are still on it. We were everywhere—from the captain's bridge to the shell hole—40 feet below decks. They even took us into one of the big gun turrets and made the loading mechanism work for us. Finally, after calling over the tannoy[46] several times, they got us all collected to take home. Our guide was a cute little Scotch sailor. We had time to eat and look over a little of the town before we got our train. There isn't any such concentrated bomb damage in London as there is there. Whole blocks flattened—it sure must have been something.

I had a very quiet weekend. I had Sat., Sunday & Monday off. Bert had Friday, Sat. & Sunday, and came up with a pass made out to Woking—20 miles from Borden—the limit. Friday night we went to see the show "Blithe Spirit." It was as good as the play—not spoiled at all. Two of the characters were the ones I had seen on the stage, although they seem to be changing all the time.

Saturday morning I went and got a permanent. Yes, at last. It is a steam affair, and very soft. They took hours to do it, and I almost took hysterics, it was so darned funny. They wound my hair with string around a rod, then put on kind of steam jackets attached to a machine. When the steam got to the end of the tube it condensed, so there were little pans hanging on the end of each one. Then somebody stalked around me with an ear syringe, and when the pans got full, glug, glug, glug went the syringe, and whoosh—into the sink. Most of the time their aim was poor, too. Anyway, it turned out well.

Saturday night was our Headquarters dance. Bert and I and Mac & Mabel and Archie went. There we met Rita and John, and Mabel and a N.Z. sailor, and Archie picked up another sailor. What a gang! During the intermission we rendered Alouette, led by John (a French-Canadian) from the beginning to the very bitter end. And they didn't even throw us out! Anyway, we all had a good time. Sunday the weather was miserable, so we didn't do a thing. Bert had to go back Sun. night. Monday Mac and Mabel and I went to Windsor. We went in the castle, but couldn't see much because the No. 1 family were in residence. We walked through Great Windsor Park, which is lovely, then down to the river (Thames). The parks all along it were nice, too. We got a train at the last minute and lucky, too, because just as we were pulling out it started to rain. We arrived back in town about 6, had supper at Bertorelli's, then home, to shine and bath.

[46] A type of public address system.

Doug is away on leave this week, but lucky for us the Winco is away, too. However, I kept busy.

Who do you think you are, Mom, not to tell me Dad was sick? Anyway, I'm glad he's better.

My draft number is 87, but that doesn't tell us a thing. Also, I just heard a happy tale that the point system for re-pat doesn't apply to Headquarters. Naturally 6 Group has folded right up and will have to be re-organized, re-trained and re-located.

Well, think I will sign off and read a little Economics or else "The Commandos." I don't think they need us much longer, which is just as well, since I'm getting tired of writing letters. Bet I've written "Gone With the Wind" and "Forever Amber" right out of the picture.

Look after yourselves until I get there to do it.

Lots of Love,

Teddy.

May 28/45.

Dear Mom & Dad:

Received your Air Mails of May 13th and 17th, and ordinary mail of the 6th, last week, all on the same day. Also got one from Marg, and one from a girl at Jarvis. Marg apparently wrote two pages of an Air Mail, and I only got the second one, so am still hoping to get the first part of the letter.

Before I forget it, will you check on my fur coat sometime when you are in Moose Jaw or Regina, or wherever it is. I wouldn't want them to think they owned it now. Hope to be wearing it this winter, maybe. Right now we have the offer of taking our discharge right now and going into UNRRA, and spending anywhere from 6 months to a year on the Continent. It would be just out of one uniform into another. The salary for clerk typists is $2000 plus accommodation. We would have to pay Canadian income tax and insurance out of it.

I don't know why you're so anxious for me to come home. You should know about how long I'll stay at Elbow—maybe 2 weeks. There isn't anywhere I'm particularly anxious to rush to. I have a good idea what I'll be like when I get back. I have had awfully good times in the service, and particularly over here, where a Canadian girl is a Goddess to the Canadian boys. I have had strange Cdn. boys come up to me and plead, "Say something—look boys, a white girl!" We have had some wild times and done a lot of crazy things—things we would never do at home. But here everyone concentrates on being a Canadian and has to demonstrate that he is more devil-may-care than the rest.

Blanche wrote me that she was quitting May 26th, but Marg said that you had written her that she would be home at the end of July. I hope she hasn't let them bully her into staying. Another summer in Washington will wear her out thoroughly. It would be nice if she were with you all summer—then you would be getting used to having your stragglers home. Blanche says she thinks the University of B.C. has improved and is all right for Arts. Too bad I don't like Toronto. I am getting a little tired of thinking about going back to school, and think it would be nice if I just got a job and started earning some money right away. There should be jobs in the East. However, I suppose I shall go right on doing what the family want, and end up a dismal failure, and they'll have to keep me in an institution in the end.

I didn't do much this week. Went to bed early every night.

Saturday the painters came to do my room. Naturally the place was a shambles. Lucky I'm not in much over the weekend. Saturday night we all went to Butch and Paul's house-warming (two boys who used to live at 55 and moved). They have a lovely big room, and it was very full of people who didn't know each other. About 10:30 the piano player from the local pub and the bar-maid arrived, and livened things up considerably. About 11 o'clock two Canadian sailors dropped in with two girls. Butch thought they were Paul's friends, and Paul thought they were Butch's, but it turned out nobody knew them, but they had a marvellous time. We danced on the boys' rug, and it was such a nice rug, too. Besides that, about 3 glasses of beer got spilled on it. Well, we went to break in the house, and we did. It turned out the bar-maid is their land-lady. We got home about 12:30, Mabel made tea, and we started looking for some place to sleep. (Incidentally, the lights are out on the second floor, and Mabel and Mac got to bed by candle-light—all very eerie). I decided to sleep in Ken Kelleway's room, since we assumed he was away for the weekend. His bed was very hard. Bert slept in Jim's bed, since we were sure he was away. (That's what I like about our house—share and share alike.) Sunday Bert and I got up at 10 o'clock and attempted to get Archie up to go to Cambridge. Archie did not get up. We got a train at 12 o'clock, and what a crawler. It stopped at every cross-road, and we got up to the Roes' about 3. She had our dinner in the oven, attempting to keep it warm. We inspected and admired the garden, visited, the men went out to inspect the re-bore job on Mr. Roe's car, had tea and it was time to leave. We got a fast train, and were making lovely time, until it was discovered that the coupling on the last car was just about not there, so we had to stop and cut it off at a siding. The tubes here were crowded, and so we didn't get to the house until 9:30.

I must quit this, and do some work.

[In handwriting] My Gosh! Here it is Thursday and this still not posted. Have been busy at work.

My room looks nice and clean—Mrs. McLean painted part of the floor around the rug tonight, so the little furniture I have put back is all in the centre. She will finish it tomorrow.

I have caught another cold, but will concentrate on getting rid of it by the weekend. Good-bye for now.

Lots of Love,
Teddy.

P.S. Got box with towel, butter and cookies. Did I tell you? Thanks a lot—the cookies were grand.

London
May 31/45.

Dear Blanche:

Didn't write to you last week, since I thought you'd be at Elbow. I have since got your letter saying you are staying and today got one of the 21st. Pretty good, eh?

. . .

Do you get a chance to vote? Our poll is open, but I haven't gone yet. The labour-progressives have posters up here, and our paper, "The Maple Leaf," runs campaign bits. Our old stand-by, the "Canadian Press News," has been dissolved and "The Maple Leaf" takes its place.

Our Winco went to Germany last week and went through the Junkers' libraries. I have been going mad typing lists of German books, pamphlets and files off his writing. He doesn't know German and, of course, I know less. It's funny about languages, though I can look at the titles, and sense somehow what they're about. Of course things like *zylinderkopfen* and *dieselmotoren* are obvious. It was fun in a way.

We have had no official word about going home. We have an offer to join UNRRA going to the continent directly, being discharged from the Air Force here. I'm going to inquire for more details.

I looked at the Sask. U. calendar here. Also got a book on elementary economics, but haven't done a lot on it—have to write too many letters. Everybody thinks I'm crazy not to get married, but of course Mom & Dad didn't sound too pleased when I broached the subject. I don't suppose I will, but it makes me mad to think they probably influenced me. Will probably spend less time at home than I would have if I had been waiting for Bert.

. . .

I am starting my leave on the 16th. Going to Ireland. We can go to Eire in civvies—not uniform. I'll probably get along well—people accuse me of sounding Irish.

I was contemplating sending you a box of food, but our rations have been cut. Just when things were getting a bit better, too. Guess it's going to the Continent. I must say the ration system here works. The prices of essentials have been kept down and if there isn't much, everybody gets a little—not the person with money getting it all.

Well, I must get to bed.

Bert 'phoned tonight to say he may not get in over the weekend, so if he doesn't I'll write you again then.

Best of everything.
Edna.

Historical Note: The United Nations Relief and Rehabilitation Administration (UNRRA) was created to provide economic assistance to European nations after World War II and to repatriate and assist the refugees who would come under Allied control.

UNRRA assisted in the repatriation of millions of refugees in 1945 and managed hundreds of displaced persons' (DPs) camps in Germany, Italy, and Austria. It provided health and welfare assistance to the DPs, as well as vocational training and entertainment.

London, Eng.
June 4/45.

Dear Mom & Dad:

I got your letter of May 23rd today, also a notice from the bank today that the money has arrived, so I must see about collecting it tomorrow noon, down on Regent Street. I didn't know Dad had bought any more land—thought he was getting rid of it.

Had a very quiet week. Mabel and I went to see "Hollywood Canteen" Tuesday night. We enjoyed it. Every once in a while we splurge on a show in the West End—six shillings—quite a splurge for just a show, isn't it?

Bert was in over the weekend. We didn't do much. Saturday night the four of us (Mabel and Mac) went to a pub in the High St. we hadn't been to before. I made coffee when we came home and we just sat and gabbed and went to bed early, and Sunday we had a lazy day.

A gang of Archie's friends, aircrew on indefinite leave before going home, are in town, and they seem to buzz in and out.

. . .

Going home seems rather distant again. We are busy even though we are over-staffed.

Mabel and I are going to Ireland on the 16th. We are going to Killarney, too. I hope another of my life-long ambitions will be realized this Sunday. We are going on an Educational tour to Salisbury and hope to get out to Stonehenge. I still hope to get to Lancashire. I have a 72 hr. pass coming in July, and think I had better go, since repat. depot is no longer up there.

Thanks a lot for the money. I haven't found out yet how much it is, but will you see that Dad takes it out of my assignment cheques, Mom? Too bad you put so much of it in the bank. I don't want the rest of the family to think you are keeping me—I'm quite capable. Haven't seen Baldy or Nicky for quite a while. Well, must write a letter to Blanche—had one from her last week. Take care of yourselves,

Love,
Teddy.

London.
June 4/45.

Dear Blanche:

Have nothing to report, but thought I'd better drop a quickie so you'll know I'm still alive. Then I must read some Economics. It's quite a change from Philosophy—a set of rules, and what is, definitely is.

This coming Sunday we are going on an Educational tour to Salisbury—Salisbury Plains, Sals. Cathedral and Stonehenge. Will try and take some pictures.

Bert was in this weekend. We had a very lazy time and did nothing except go out to the pub Saturday night. The A.O.C. in C. is strolling around these days looking for people writing personal letters, and posting them "Elsewhere." "Elsewhere" being the East, so the Winco came out today to see what was going on in the Orderly Room. He started snooping around in the cupboard, found some drawings a month old and proceeded to blow his top.

. . .

I don't think I ever told you about the bracelet I had given to me. It is one of those wide silver clip-on ones. It has a silver heart soldered on the front, with engraving at the sides. The heart has "Edna 1945" on it, and at one side is "Canada," and the other "England." It is very nice. I wear it all the time, but haven't been checked on it. They are pretty easy-going over here.

. . .

I don't think I'll take that trip to Europe with you. I'm going to see all I can while I'm here, and then quit. Going to see the Continent if I have to stow away.

Well, as I said, there is no news. Haven't seen Reimer. Will sign off now and spend some time on Economics.

So long, Love
Edna.

[Post card of O'Connell Bridge and Street, Dublin, postmarked 19 June 1945]
Dear Mom & Dad:

Having a wonderful luxurious time in Dublin—the city without a war. It is really swell—wish we had more time here. Probably my letter of next week will reach you before this, but this will give you an idea of the city's centre. Wish you could see it. Lots of love,
Teddy.

June 25th.

Dear Family:

So what if this is a carbon copy? You're lucky to get that. The purpose of it is to tell everybody everything about my leave all at once. Well, it was simply marvellous. There is no war in Ireland and they have everything—

especially food. I had a complete set of hives by Sunday night, and by Monday they were the most beautiful collection I have ever seen.

Mabel and I just made the train last Saturday morning, with the help of a slow taxi. We got a seat after a while. The train trip was very dull and uneventful. Mac had made sandwiches for our lunch the night before. Good old Mac! We got on the train at 8 o'clock in the morning and arrived at Holyhead about 2:30. It took two hours to get through Customs, passes checked, etc. By the way, we can't go into Eire in uniform—Dev[47] hasn't told them yet there's a war on. I travelled in my kilt, and it is the clear rig. No matter how long I sit it doesn't get mussed, being hard material, and doesn't show any dust or dirt. Took skirt and blouse, and slacks and sweater, and dress. We finally got on the boat, but they didn't get everybody on and started until 6 o'clock. We arrived at the harbor—Dunloarghie (pronounced Dun Larrie) about 9, and got through the Irish customs in short order. Well, then there is about a 15 minute train ride to Dublin. When we arrived, we went to our hotel, cleaned up, then went to the dining room for supper—ham and eggs. What a treat!

Sunday we looked in the store windows, also a treat, and went out to Phoenix Park. It is a huge park, and well kept. We visited the Zoo in it. It wasn't as good as Regent's Park Zoo. Sunday night we took it easy, and went to bed. We treated ourselves to numerous ice cream sundaes throughout our stay in Dublin. Monday we went on a shopping spree. It was a good thing clothes are on coupons there, too. As it was, I bought a small alarm clock, a fountain pen, some lovely leather gloves, post cards and souvenirs.

We went to the Tourist Association and got advice about going to Killarney. We got a bus at 8 o'clock Tuesday morning and arrived at Cork at a quarter to 5. It was a nice run, and the country is lovely. We got a bus right away to Killarney—another 3 hours' run. We arrived there about 8:30, and get this—there were about 8 hotel porters around the bus <u>coaxing</u> people to come to their hotel. We went to the Glebe, and it was a lucky choice. There were a lot of service people there—Aussies and Canadians. There were 5 of us—Mabel and I and two other girls we knew from Headquarters, and F/L Collins whom I used to work for at Jarvis. Imagine him popping up!

It is a small hotel, so very friendly. I shot the head porter a lot of blarney and could just about get what we wanted. He really looked after us. The dining room was open until all hours, and the food was even better than in Dublin. Boy! Ham and eggs and steaks, and salmon steaks! It wasn't expensive either. Well, the first night we were there I thought I saw a familiar face in the bar, and it turned out to be a friend of Archie's. Of all the service

---

[47] Eamon De Valera, one of the leaders of the Easter Rising of 1916, became president of the Irish Free State in 1932 and subsequently prime minister and president of the Irish Republic, or Eire. Ireland remained officially neutral during World War II.

people, about every second one was A.W.L.[48] No military camps, and no S.P.[49] Besides there was a doctor there who would give you a certificate to say you were sick for 5 shillings. Of course, all the sickness was digestive trouble and dysentery. We would have stayed, but couldn't afford to.

We intended to go on a long tour right up to the upper lake and back down on Wednesday, and go back Thursday, but it rained Wed. There are only 4 trains a week in and out of the place. It quit raining Wednesday noon, so we took a trip by jaunting car—(a two-wheeled one-horse affair—wait until you see a picture—I can't describe it) about 15 miles around the lower and middle lakes. We got back about 5:30, and didn't want to eat dinner yet, so Jimmy (head porter) opened up the ballroom and got out the ping-pong bats, and even opened up the piano. I got beat two rousing games of ping-pong, but then Bill beat everybody else too, so I didn't feel so bad.

Oh, I forgot to tell you. Wednesday morning we went to two convents in pouring rain to look at their lace. The nuns make it to sell, and it is really beautiful. I got a pair of lovely fine doilies—the beginning of my hopeful chest. Although Killarney is only a small town, they have a huge Cathedral and two convents. There the R.C. is the State Church—same as Church of England here. Also got a fine muslin hanky with about an inch of hand-made lace around it.

Well, to get back to Wednesday night. After dinner Mabel and I were sitting in the lounge thinking it was going to be a dull evening, when Harry, a Canadian sailor, who is about a week A.W.L., came in to ask if we would go and have a drink with his friend the padre. He turns out to be the cutest Irish priest with dimples. By the time we have a couple of beers with him, all the rest of the gang had come into the bar, and the priest left. Well, people kept drifting in until the place was full. About 11 o'clock we all went in a body to another hotel, and stayed there until they kicked us out. Then we came back to the Glebe, settled down in one of the small lounges. We lit the peat fire in the fire-place, and a couple of local men that happened to be there sung us Irish songs. They were really beautiful. Mabel and I went to bed about 3 o'clock, and on the way upstairs changed the shoes standing outside the doors around. The boys stayed up until 7 o'clock.

The next morning was fine, and so we decided to stay and go on the long trip. It turned out we didn't have to go A.W.L. because there was a train Thursday night. We started out about 11 o'clock by horse cart. After a two hour ride we arrived at the Gap of Dunloe, which is the pass through the mountains between the upper and middle lakes. We climbed on to horses there. You know my horse experience? Well, the boys thought I had lots of nerve, but I couldn't walk for 6 miles. The mountains through the pass are

[48] Away without leave
[49] Special Police

Tour of Killarney, June 1945.

rocky and wild, and the scenery beautiful, although I wish I could have given more attention to it. Well, anyway, I arrived at the head of the upper lake third, so I showed, at least. There is a cottage there where we ate the lunch the hotel had packed for us.

Then we started out by boat. There were 14 or 16 of us in this big row-boat with 4 men to paddle. One was young, and as we came down the lakes he told us all the legends connected with them. They are varied and colorful, and lost nothing in the telling. We arrived at Ross castle, at the bottom of the lower lake, about 5:30, and went back to town (about 2 miles) by horse cart again.

We then rushed to the hotel, had dinner and got to the station for the train. It consisted of two baggage cars and one passenger coach. However, passengers were few, so we got a seat to Mallow, where we changed to a real train. By the time we arrived it was packed, so the boys gave the trainman 2 shillings, and we moved into a baggage coach. At least it had two seats. There were four of us girls, an RCAF boy from London, and an RAF chap. One of them stretched out on the floor and slept nearly all the way. We stopped at Limerick for half an hour in the middle of the night, but got out and went to the Refreshment Room which was open. We had some chicken sandwiches the hotel packed for us.

Well, we arrived at Dublin about 5:30, tuckered right out. We had kept our hotel room, so we turned right in. May and Millie hadn't, and couldn't get in their room right away, so they came in and laid on one of our beds. As soon as the hot water was on (7 o'clock), I had a bath, the girls got into their room, and we went to bed. We slept until 1:30, when we got up and started to collect ourselves.

We had asked for an estimate of our bill for the week, and she said about £5 each. We discovered that we didn't have £10 between us, and had a very uncomfortable afternoon, and didn't do any more shopping, although we decided we deserved a big sundae to keep our morale up. We thought of every means or getting money, and none of them would work. Millie and May had gone out and done a lot of shopping and didn't have any surplus. Well, we couldn't stand the suspense any longer and finally asked for our bill. Luckily it was less, and we had just enough to pay it.

Well, Saturday morning we were really mad. We wanted to make the first boat-train, which was 25 to 7. At 6:30 the girls called us to tell us the taxi was there. We got out of bed, didn't wash or clean our teeth or even comb our hair. We rushed down-stairs, looked about 5 minutes for the night porter, gave him hell, and he said our call and our taxi order had been crossed out of the call book. Well, anyway, he got us a taxi and we made the second train. We got through Customs pretty fast, and managed to get breakfast on the boat. The trip was rather rough, but uneventful.

The boys were supposed to meet us at Euston at 9 o'clock, but as we got in half an hour early, we went out for supper, felling pretty smart because we still had about 6 shillings left. When we went to pay our bill, the girl said, "Sorry, we can't take Irish money." We didn't have enough English money to make it up.

We went back to the station to find the boys, and oddly enough didn't have trouble finding them. We went home. The boys had a big bouquet of flowers in each of our rooms. I guess they were really lost while we were away. The first weekend they went to the dog races.

We sat up late Saturday night, and slept in late Sunday. It was a beautiful day, but we just felt lazy and laid down in the sun—we see so little of it. Bert and Mac didn't have any money either, but Mac had groceries in, so the two of them cooked supper for us Sunday. It was quite a treat—we said they could do it all the time.

Bert had to leave about 9:30, so we considered we had a very good weekend after our leave. We certainly liked Ireland. Maybe the food influenced us, but we liked the people, too. The trouble is that you see terrible slums in the cities and mud hovels in the country—all with dozens of kids. Then there will be an estate of thousands of acres owned by one man. We were in Dublin on election night (for the president) and didn't even notice any more commotion than usual. There is an Irish army. They wear olive drab uniforms with high necks—just like the Germans. They are starting to demob them with high gratuities, and they haven't done anything—except run the election and put on a tattoo. Maybe you don't realize it, but the German envoy is still living outside Dublin.

Well, this is all I can think of right now—probably will think of little bits in later letters. Took two rolls of snaps and will send them when I get them developed.

Must sign off and do some work.
Love,
Teddy.

July 4.

Dear Mom & Dad:

Got your Air Mail this week. Hope Grandpa is well enough now for you to be home. Has Dad started his month's holiday yet that Blanche said he was taking? In connection with that holiday, I must have words with you. You didn't say Dad was sick—just not well, and Blanche had to tell me he really was sick. You had better tell me a few things in the future, and here's why:—I put in my application to go to the Continent with UNRRA for a year. Of course, I wouldn't have done it if I had known Dad was sick. Luckily, I was turned down, but you can see what might have happened. You can just loosen up in the future. After all, you'd hear soon enough if I got seriously ill, but I wouldn't hear about you.

This is my new pen I got in Ireland. It's an Ingersoll, and pretty good. Incidentally, anything you bring back from there is smuggled, but guess I got practice going to the States.

Didn't do much last week. Bert got in Saturday morning since he has been working nights and got Sat. morning off. . .

Mac and Bert had Monday off. We did, too, technically, but both Mabel and I had to go to church parade. However, we got the boys up when we got up—8 o'clock. Bert shone my shoes and buttons as I ate breakfast.

The parade was our Dominion Day celebration. There were hundreds of Canadians—Navy, Army and Air Force. We started at Wellington Barracks (the famous home of the Guards), went up the Mall to Trafalgar Square, then down Whitehall to Westminster Abbey. The R.C.'s went on to Westminster Cathedral. Mac went down to the Cathedral, but no one else could get in the Abbey. The King and Queen and Elizabeth came to the service, but I didn't see them—too many people in front of me. The Archbishop of York gave the sermon—he talked through his nose, and the acoustics were poor. Also there was a clock right in the church that struck the quarter hours and kept waking me up.

Anyway, they got a Canadian flag consecrated, and we got out about 1 o'clock. We met Mabel and Mac and went to Bertorelli's, and ate a huge dinner we were all so hungry. Then we went home and slept, just like pigs. I made supper, and Bert had to leave early. I got to bed in fair time. Sure hated to come back to work Tuesday morning. One of the padres asked for us to have time off to compensate for going on parade, but his (C.O.'s) reply was that the honor should compensate us. I didn't see any honor floating around—I would rather have had something more concrete.

Last night I did my laundry. This morning the 'phone rang about 7 o'clock, and who should it be but Bill Johnson—Doris's husband. He just flew in from Africa. Mrs. MacLean has a bed to put him up—he is here for 3 weeks. Don't know where he has disappeared to tonight, but I imagine he'll amuse himself alright. His tour was cut short about 2 months, so I bet Jack Woods will be back earlier than he expected, too. I told Jack if he thought I was going to stay in England until October just to see him, he was crazy.

I got a letter from Elmer in England, but it was slow coming, so don't know if he's still here or not. Also got one from Barney—guess he'll be home on leave soon. My hives are almost better—the English diet. Last week I could hardly eat at all.

I am going to see if I can send some money home right away—the pound is going down further in dollar value—$4.03 I think it's going to—and after all, our pay is on a dollar basis. I don't want to lose money on the pounds I have.

. . .

Well, must sign off and write to Dorothy. I got her parcel. Also a box of candy from Blanche.
'Bye now,
Lots of love,
Teddy.

July 4.

Dear Blanche:

Got the box of fudge this week. Thanks ever so much—we all enjoyed it. The office staff don't believe it when I tell them you can't cook.

Well, this is election eve. There has been more dirt-slinging, lawsuits, accusations and insults than we ever have at home. One thing I notice, though. They don't dig up their opponents' past shady life or ever refer to their families (except of course Mr. Churchill's son-in-law, Duncan Sandys[50]). The Socialists were strong enough, but I think have definitely lost by their split. The people still adore Churchill for his war record. The opposition made a mistake by forcing the election now.

Nominally, Monday was a holiday for us, but some of us had to go on church parade. It was a good big parade—we treated London to the sight of

---

[50] Duncan Sandys (1908–87), British politician and statesman who exerted major influence on foreign and domestic policy during mid-twentieth-century Conservative administrations.

hundreds of Canadians at once—Navy, Army & Air Force. We started at Wellington Barracks, marched up the Mall to Admiralty Arch. Mr. Massey and the Missus took the salute on the march past. We all felt sorry for old weasel face, with his bald head exposed to the weather, while the Mrs. dripped furs. We went through Trafalgar Square and then down Whitehall to Westminister Abbey. An English Church Service after all that marching! You know how much you stand in one. The King & Queen & Lizzie junior came, but I couldn't see them. I didn't enjoy the service particularly:—

1. The man who chanted the psalms sang through his nose.
2. C of E hymns are deadly.
3. The Archbishop of York gave the sermon, but the acoustics are as bad as the seating in the Abbey.
4. The place is always cold & damp.
5. There was a clock behind me which struck the quarter hours and kept me awake.

. . .

I wish we'd get some sun. About 3 weeks ago we had a nice Sunday, and I hopefully started a tan, but it must be all faded by now. It has been cold and wet.

Speaking of Eisenhower, they really went crazy over him here. In fact, he was made an honorary citizen of London.

They must send all the RAF with a sense of humor to Washington. You should see the ghouls that wander around Kingsway. Long, lean mournful-looking men that wander up and down with their hands clasped behind their back, in usual warlike RAF appearance. . . .

I was also surprised about our election. I had to vote in Regina constituency, but don't know who got in.

Last week Pauline was away, and Doug and I were terribly busy, and this week it is the same. Today the major ordered me back to D.A.S. saying I was only supposed to be on loan to Engineering. Well, I'll get a rest in D.A.S., anyway. By the way, the Groupie I worked for at the D.A.S. is now an A/C, and is Deputy A.O.C. Our former D.-A.O.C. is going to the East.

Isn't is nice to read in the papers the names of the troopships and when they will dock? No word of our repat. yet. Our "R" Depot has been moved to Torquay, a lovely summer resort, so hope we make it while the weather is decent.

I must sign off, as Archie should be finished pressing his uniform, and I want to press the undies I washed last night.

Love,
Edna

Historical Notes: Despite Churchill's impressive leadership as prime minister during the war years and his immense popularity amongst the British people, voters opted for a new outlook as they embraced peace. Clement Atlee and the Labour Party won the general election of July 1945 over Churchill and the Conservative Party to form a majority government. This was the first general election to be held in Great Britain since 1935, as general elections had been suspended during the war. It also took nearly a month to determine the results as votes had to be collected from service people posted overseas.

However, in Canada the month before, the status quo prevailed when William Lyon Mackenzie King and the Liberals were elected to their third consecutive majority on June 11. This took some observers by surprise, as this was the first general election since the CCF had won in Saskatchewan and many had predicted the party to break through nationally. Some even went so far as to suggest that the socialists could form a minority government.

Vincent Massey served as Canada's high commissioner to the United Kingdom from 1935 until 1946. In 1952, he became Canada's first native-born governor general.

Dwight D. Eisenhower, Supreme Commander, Allied Expeditionary Forces, commanded the forces of the Normandy invasion. His tremendous popularity helped earn him two terms as president of the United States (1953–61).

July 9, 1945.

Dear Mom & Dad:

How is the weather and the crops etc? We have had four days of sunshine, now, and it is really nice for a change. We actually laid out in the court in bathing suits. I haven't got a tan yet, but perhaps have the start of one, if we get any more sun.

Didn't do much all week. Thursday I went on X-ray parade. They are doing everybody in Headquarters, because a few cases of T.B. have been discovered, I guess.

The major in D.A.S. kicked last week because I was supposed to belong to them, and he suddenly remembered that I had only been loaned to Engineering, so nothing would do but I had to come back. So here I am. The W/C has phoned once this morning, presumably to put in a kick, but no one has said anything to me yet.

Tuesday [in handwriting]

Gee, it really poured rain this morning. It's still warm though.

I haven't heard from you since the last time I wrote, so haven't much to say.

They miss me sadly in Engineering. This D.A.S. Orderly Room is the same as ever, but I guess I'll get used to it. The W/C I work for seems quite nice—the same one I was supposed to work for when I was here before. The boy he had has now been posted, so I'm afraid Engineering will have to do some strong kicking to get me back. I don't give a darn where I work, or if I do, at this stage.

Everybody is restless these days. Things are dull, and nothing happens.

I got a parcel form Dorothy today, but haven't opened it yet.

Tonight Kath and I are going to try to get in the D'Oly Carte opera—"The Gondeliers." I managed to get tickets for next Tuesday for "Yeoman of the Guard."

We had a very lazy weekend. Saturday morning we just about went crazy in the office—we had two deputations over from Canada and had to arrange transportation, etc., for where they wanted to go. Bert had Saturday morning off (he worked Friday night) so was in at 1 o'clock. We meandered home. I cleaned up, and we went out for supper. Sunday we had breakfast about 1, and laid outside in the sun. I cooked dinner and washed the dishes, then Bert had to go. I shone my buttons & shoes, and was just about ready for bed when Archie came in. We sat on his floor, made toast and ate shrimps, then I finally got to bed. Must sign off now and do some converting of this desk to my own liking.

Lots of love,
Teddy.

July 16, 45.

Dear Mom, Dad & Blanche:

First, I intended to write Blanche one more letter to Washington, counting on her being there until July 31, but decided I had better not when I discovered she was leaving on the 25th. I don't envy her spending 2 days in New York in July. Besides that, I just read in this morning's paper where people are asked to make their own beds, because all the chamber-maids have left New York for the summer.

Last Tuesday Kath and I went to see "Iolanthe." It was quite good. I enjoyed it because it was a new one to me. I'm catching up on Gilbert and Sullivan gradually, though.

I was tired all week from the weekend before, so endeavored to get to bed early a couple of nights. Wednesday night I did my laundry. Thursday night I washed my hair and went across the street to the pub with Bill [Johnson], since it was his last night. He has left for the holding unit at Brighton. He will be two months in Canada, and is hoping Doris can get discharged so she can go to New Zealand with him. Friday night I did my ironing.

Bert came in Saturday afternoon. We had tea, laid out in the sun, and then the four of us went to Bertorelli's for supper. We couldn't decide what to do with the rest of the evening, so went to an old hang-out

Bert and Edna and Mabel and Mac in front of their local, the Crown and Sceptre.

we haven't been to for quite a while—The Warwick Arms. On our way home we popped into the Crown & Sceptre to see who was there. We got home early—about 8:30. We sat and gabbed in my room then I made tea. Mac brought his radio down so we also listened to Jack Benny and various dance bands until 12 o'clock, when the B.B.C. shuts down. Then I took a bath. We put our clocks back Saturday night, and are now on 1 hour summer time instead of two. Sunday night they therefore put the street lights on, and they really look swell. In the Spring before we went on daylight-saving they didn't have them all on, but now they are really almost pre-war.

Sunday morning was beautiful, almost like July at home. After we had breakfast (about 12:30), we decided we were tired of the city and wanted to look at some country, so we got on a bus and rode to the edge of town (1 hour's ride), walked a little ways, and there we were. At least there were a few open fields. It clouded up, so we started back for the bus, and just got on when it started to rain, and it really poured. It stopped just before we got back to Shepherd's Bush.

Saturday night we had a real thunder and lightning storm—unusual here. Quite a few things were struck. Well, anyway, when we got home Sunday night we just had supper and Bert had to go. I just shined and washed and went to bed.

I got a parcel from Blanche on Saturday—the one with the lipstick and rouge and cream in it. Thanks a lot, I think the lipstick is glamorous. I use rouge very seldom, but it will do for special occasions. I have a very nice natural color now, and my complexion is much nicer than it was in Canada. I always knew English girls only got that way from the climate. I can see Blanche rushing right over.

It's nice to see the ships that are going and when they land in the papers now. I'll bet Halifax must be going mad. I really don't expect to be on one before September.

I got a parcel from Dorothy last week—or did I tell you?

I used to think Engineering reports were complicated to take in shorthand, but Saturday morning I did one for a visiting Photography W/C, and it took the cake. If I ever went back to just doing straight business letters it would seem funny.

Tuesday Afternoon

Have been moderately busy up to now, for a change. It is warm again today. You never know what this country is going to do next—yesterday it was cold.

I wish Blanche would get over here before I left. I would like to show her London at least.

Got an Air Mail from you yesterday afternoon. I am glad the crop is alright now, so that means another winter at the Coast for you. Aren't you going to the Beach? I thought Blanche said you were.

Barney should be home, too, as I understand all the Army going to the Pacific are supposed to have left here. I don't know what squadron Art was on, but he must have been on one of those that are going East as a squadron, and flew to Canada. They will be there a little while.

Well, I can't think of any news, because nothing happens. We are going to have a quiet weekend this week, and the next one we are going to the Isle of Wight.

So long for now—
Love,
Edna.

On another occasion at the Warwick Arms, Mac bought two cigars, and Doris asked where was hers. Mac got her one and she lit up. Customers around the pub buzzed, and I told the lady beside me that she had one often. The story got back to the other side of me that she "had one every day."

In July 1945, Blanche quit her job in Washington with the British Air Commission for a number of reasons: it had a lot of stress, the summer heat in Washington was unbearable, and her office had mostly finished programming the attack on Japan. And as our father was not well, and most of the boys had enlisted by now, Blanche returned to the farm near Elbow, where she did business for him, including accounting and whatnot, but mostly chauffeuring him about. The farm was six miles from Elbow and eighty miles from Saskatoon, where we had to go for machine repairs. He passed away in 1948.

July 23/45.

Dear Blanche and Family:

Received your letters of the 9th and 10th, Blanche. Sorry you haven't been getting mail from me. I wrote a giant letter about Ireland—hope the rest of the family got theirs. I wrote the last letter to Blanche two weeks ago.

Kath said to thank you for the stamps. Hope she keeps them hidden from the Winco—he nabs off every stamp that comes into the office.

I am still in the D.A.S. Orderly Room—not doing much of anything.

London is quite gay with the lights on. Now if rationing would only quit, it would be quite the normal city. It hasn't let up a bit, and in fact some things seem to get worse. We used to get an egg quite regularly once a week, but haven't had one this month yet. Oh well, maybe our store will get several allocations in at once. As for soap—well, the ration, small as it is, is very hard to find. I manage to get along, because somebody always thinks to put soap in a parcel, but if you want to please any of your other friends in England, send them some.

The main event last week was a young man, only 24 mind you, copping the heavy-weight title from Jack London. All the news issued from Potsdam is a list of what they are eating and drinking, and London reads the paper drooling. Papers have got much more local news nowadays—a murder even makes the front page now. A bunch of men have got disgusted with the Ministry of Housing and are taking over houses by force and installing army wives and widows in them. They call themselves the Vigilantes, and have the local councils worried.

I haven't done much exciting. Last week I went to see the Dough Girls at Warner's on Leicester Square. I really enjoyed it—haven't laughed so much in a show for a long time.

Bert was on a 48, so he came in on Friday night. We tried to get into a show, but couldn't, so the four of us (Mabel and Mac) went to the Crown and Sceptre (to see Mrs. Morris). Mrs. Morris is a local institution in our neighbourhood. She and her husband keep the local pub, and therefore are well known. She takes an interest in everyone's private life, and cringes every time our gang comes in.

We came home, and I made tea. Mabel and Mac were on a 48 and went to Canterbury Saturday morning. Bert met me at 1 o'clock Saturday and I took him to the Churchill Club for lunch. We went out and shopped, I made tea, and then we went to see "To Have and Have Not." We enjoyed it, but I didn't realize the theatre was as far as it turned out to be, and it seemed that we walked miles. We got home about 10, and had supper on the floor—asparagus with cheese sauce on toast, and toast and jam. What is more, I made it! I still can't figure out how one really ought to make cheese sauce, but what I made tasted good, anyway. Bert shone my buttons while I took a bath, and I at last got to bed.

Sunday morning we got up in time to get the Dover train at 11 o'clock. Yes, we even got up in time to have breakfast. We stood all the way to Dover—2? hours. Mabel and Mac met us at the station, and we went in search of a place to eat. After we had dinner, we started looking for the cliffs. We walked towards a street that went up. After walking up for a while, we climbed about 100 steps, then walked some more just about straight up, and finally got up on top. It is just like an army camp—in fact it is, but like almost all camps here, you are right in the middle of them before you realise they are there. Anyway, we climbed in and out of gun emplacements, scrambled up hillocks, etc., in order to see everything in the harbor, and we didn't miss anything since we had a pair of binoculars. Saw a B.L.A. boat coming in, among other things. It was a beautiful day, and we were sorry we didn't have longer to stay, to walk further along the cliff. We got a fast train back, and a seat. Arrived about 8, and Mabel cooked up supper—beans and spam and toast. Then Bert had to leave.

He starts leave tonight, and is going to Scotland until Friday. I am going down to Waterloo to meet him, since he has a couple of hours until the Flying Scotsman leaves. He hasn't been up to see his cousin for 6 months, since he spent his last leave in London. Next Saturday we are going to the Isle of Wight, and he will have until Wednesday in town.

Well, it is almost 5:30, and I can't think of anything else to say, however I will leave this until tomorrow morning.

Tuesday

I almost forgot to tell you the most important thing—I saw France (through binoculars). The rest of the kids say all they saw was a smudge of cliffs, but I definitely saw a man talking with his hands, and a sign that said "Cap Grenier—turn left for Pierre's Horseburgers."

Love,
Teddy.

Historical Note: At the Potsdam Conference of July 17 to August 2, 1945, Britain, Russia, and the United States met to clarify and implement agreements reached at Yalta a few months earlier. Potsdam divided post-war Germany into four occupation zones and reorganized Germany's institutions and economy. The Allies also called for Japan to surrender or risk total destruction.

August 1/45.

Dear Mom & Dad & Blanche:

Heaven knows where you all are, but I hope you are having a nice holiday at the Beach.

. . .

Bert came back from Scotland Friday night, and Saturday morning we started out for I. of W. According to the time-table it takes 4 hours, but it took us all day. We would have to pick the worst day in the history of crowds—all going to the Isle of Wight. We stood in line for two hours for a train—not being able to get on two. When we got to Portsmouth there were a lot of people ahead of us, and we waited for a boat for four hours—standing in line. We didn't get on about four boats. Well, we finally got to Ryde about 7:30, and got a train right to Shanklin, the town where we were staying—on the other side of the island. Of course you know how small the Isle of Wight is. We got accommodation through Auxiliary Services at a guest house. The lady was swell to us and insisted we come back. It was cheap, too, for a summer resort at the peak of its season.

When we arrived Saturday night high tea was waiting for us. We then went out and looked over the town. It is primarily a summer resort, but all the hotels along the beach are absolutely battered beyond repair. The beach goes right along the coast and is lovely fine sand—most of the beaches on the south coast of England are pebbles or shale. Something (no doubt the sea air) made us terribly sleepy, so we came home and went to bed. Sunday was a beautiful day, and we got up for breakfast (9 o'clock) and went down to the beach. I was sorry I didn't put on my bathing suit, but we paddled about 2 miles down the beach, then sat and leaned against the cliff—it was beautiful to be lazy. We got back in time to have a beer and wash before dinner. Then we put on our bathing suits and went back to the beach. We laid in the sun for a while and then, get this—I went in the sea! I guess it's about time, considering the length of time I've been here. It wasn't much colder than a lake, but I imagine would have been to stay in very long. We were chilly when we came out, so went and got dressed and lounged around until suppertime. After supper we walked around town and sat a while in a pub, then home to bed.

Monday was rather grey and cloudy, so we walked through the old village. It is really pretty, set in kind of a gully, and all the houses have thatched roofs. Then next to it is a kind of settlement (wouldn't call it a village) called Chine. It is in a rift between the cliffs, although on top of the cliffs—kind of a fault—and has lovely big trees and a waterfall. It is really lovely. We left Shanklin about 3:30 to go to Ryde. We had time to have a look at the main street and have tea before we got the boat. It wasn't terribly crowded, thank goodness. We didn't get a train at Portsmouth harbour—we had to go downtown, but got one right away. Got back to London about 8:30. Altogether we had a swell weekend, and even think it was worth the trouble getting down. We are going again August 25th and taking Mabel and Mac with us.

Bert met me for lunch Tuesday and Wednesday, then Wednesday night he went back to camp.

This weekend is August Bank Holiday—when the whole country goes on holiday at once. It is the craziest system I have ever heard of. In the paper this morning it said there were just not enough trains for everybody—because everyone goes to the Sea.

I don't know why they don't smarten up. As Kay said yesterday—anything stupid in England they blame on tradition, and anything stupid in Canada they blame on women.

. . .

Yesterday noon there was an exhibition tennis match between our champ and the American champ—it was a good game—nice to watch. Well, they were still playing at a quarter to 2, so I left to come back to work, and Bert stayed to watch. I had nicely got settled down at my typewriter when in comes the Major—"Look what I found outside!"—with Bert in tow. They knew each other in Ottawa, and after me carefully depositing Bert outside, the Major insisted he come up. Well, with not even half trying the Major said I could get off early—he was in a good mood and wanted to show himself as a good guy. So I left about 4 o'clock. We took Bert's bag to Waterloo, then went out to Shepherd's Bush to Bertorelli's, then home. Bert shone my buttons and I did my shoes. By the time we had a little visit with Archie, it was time for Bert to go. I washed and put up my hair, and fell into bed at 9 o'clock, thoroughly exhausted. I went right off to sleep, being wakened only at 9:30 by Mrs. MacLean with tea, because she didn't know I was in bed. I felt fresh as a daisy this morning, but to-night have to do a washing I should have done last night.

This weekend is going to be quiet—not only because we don't feel like doing much after the way we have been rushing around, but because anyone who tries to travel and doesn't have to must be nuts.

Well, I can't think of much more to say.

Oh yes, yesterday just after I left, Jack Woods came up looking for me. He left town last night but would be back in a week, so after expecting him for so long I missed him. He must have lost my home phone number.

Well, look after yourselves.

Lots of Love,

Teddy.

August 8/45.

Dear Mom, Dad & Blanche:

Received your letter of July 22nd yesterday, also Blanche's of the 23rd and card from New York, and letter from Marg of the 29th (Air Mail).

Yes, mother dear, you're not the only one who thinks I won't be home for a while. Probably either October, or else not until March. After a long while, the big boys got to thinking what to do with the W.D.'s, and when it got down to the fine thing, they decided they can't do without us. In fact, yesterday's Maple Leaf says that Gibson wants to send us to the East. I'd like to go East, but after arguing Bert out of it I'd better let well enough alone. . . I hope you get to the Beach—if only for the sake of getting a roof on the toilet.

I think I told you last week how I missed Jack Woods, but he would be in town again any day now.

I haven't been doing much. This Monday was the famous English Bank Holiday, when everybody tramples everybody else to get to the sea—we stayed home, although we got Monday off. I was duty clerk Saturday afternoon and had to work until about 4 o'clock. Naturally Bert was home when I got there. We sat and gabbed in Mabel's room—Jim telling us his experiences in a Roman Catholic school for boys in Winnipeg. Then Mabel and I changed into civvies and we went to Bertorelli's for supper. We had a quiet evening.

Sunday we got up about 9, had a leisurely breakfast while Mac and Mabel went to church, then we packed a lunch and went to Hampstead Heath for a picnic. This Heath is actually in London, but is really big and just like country. We got off the bus right beside a pub called the Olde Bull and Bush, so we had to investigate. It was built with a new brick front, but the building was really old. Low ceilings with big black beams. There was a parrot sitting there, and Mabel said, "That parrot almost looks real." I turned around to look, whereupon it opened its eyes, solemnly winked at me, and closed them again, very bored. Anyway, we proceeded across the Heath and found a place to park. We promptly flopped to read the Sunday papers and dirt sheets, and after a while got up enough energy to eat. After that Mac saw how many trees he could climb and chased Mabel around in her stocking feet, then we went home. I cooked dinner again—quite domestic, aren't I. Then Bert had to leave, since he didn't have Monday off.

I had a beautiful lazy day Monday—slept until 11 o'clock, did a laundry, washed my hair, then went out to try and get some supper—since I hadn't bothered to eat all day. Just got to the door at Bertorelli's when they closed, so I decided to go to a show instead. I stood in line there for half an hour, and finally got in to see "I'll be Seeing You." I enjoyed it. Went home, had some toast and milk and went to bed.

About the biggest event of the week is that we don't have parades any more—just the C.O.'s parade once a week. What is more, we don't have to go to work until 9 o'clock, have an hour and half at noon, and quit at 5 o'clock. They say it is for "health reasons," and I said to myself bitterly, it took 17 cases of T.B. to wake them up.

One of our runners is going home Saturday, so he insisted in taking us all out last night for a beer. Lucky I had to leave early because Johnny Brown, one of Doris's old flames, was coming up. When he arrived, he and I and Mabel and Mac went to see "National Velvet." I thought it wasn't extraordinary. By the time he left and I got to bed it was 12:30. To-night I hope to get to bed, although I have to iron and press and take a bath and should put up my hair.

The present news taking up all the front pages is the new bomb. The first reaction was "Good for them," but today when it came out that 30,000 were killed and a whole city wiped out, it seems rather horrible, and I think people are a little aghast at what we have done. Tony, our "Red" runner, was in this morning delivering a lecture to all and sundry on the evils of it. He is the one who is all out for the civilizing of Limehouse—he thinks it would be cleaned up if they gave the people any money. All this in spite of the fact that it has been proved that if you give the lower classes bath-tubs, they only use them to keep coal in.

Oh, mom, Blanche is complaining because she doesn't know where I sailed from—you'll tell her all the details of my trip over, etc. We will be arriving back at Halifax, or maybe Quebec, because of the congestion in rail traffic. One thing I am sure of, and that is that I won't be returning on the same boat I came on, for a very simple reason.[51]

---

[51] I had sailed over to England in the *Empress of Japan*, which was renamed the *Empress of Scotland* after Japan entered the war.

Well, I have a terrible time thinking of new things to tell you, and have said just about everything now. Must sign off.

Regards to all,

Teddy.

August 14th/45.

Dear Mom, Dad & Blanche:

Received your letter of July 30th last week, and Blanche's from Mt. Brydges of July 31st yesterday.

I think I forgot to tell Blanche that I got the parcel with the Rice Krispie candy in it. It was very good, and we all enjoyed it. Thanks also for the bars, etc.

I hope you got some rain to save the crop. Maybe you will get cured of farming yet.

Doug Johnstone went to the hospital last week, so once again the Wing Commander had to ask to have me back in Engineering while he is away. They just can't get along without me. So far I have got along with the Wingco without coming to blows. Maybe it is because I don't worry about the work, therefore he doesn't bother me when he gets in a flap. I do what he wants, but without acting as if I were ready to spring when he wants me. Shouldn't be very long here, though.

Mrs. MacLean's son is home from school for six weeks, so I moved up with Mabel to give him my room. Had a little argument with her about the rent, but got it settled. On the first floor there is Mabel and I in one big room, and Mac and Jim in a big room and a small room, so we have the whole floor to ourselves, and Jim isn't in very much. Bert was in over the weekend, but didn't do much and it was very quiet.

Friday 17th

Sorry this is still not away, but we had a holiday Wednesday and Thursday,[52] and I have been very busy today. Bert came in Wednesday afternoon (unofficially), since their Colonel got drunk and in a spell of magnaminxxx (oh, let it go—in a spell anyway) let them off for the afternoon, against Headquarters' wishes. He had to go back at night, but we put in a little celebrating. We were afraid to go down to the West End, because we remember walking home on VE night. Thursday I had a quiet day—ironing, etc. Thursday night Bert came in with a pass for four days. We are going to Isle of Wight tomorrow.

Got your letter of August 6 today. Glad Blanche is looking well after all our worry about her. You're sure the bomber crashing into the Empire State

---

[52] To celebrate victory in the Pacific, VJ Day.

Building didn't hurt her? Frankly, all that fuss makes me sick. Not that I'd want all our buildings knocked down like they are here.

Is Blanche going out to the Coast, staying at the farm, or what?

Not a word about us going home. Bert thinks now he may be home by October. What do you mean—how can I plan on getting married while I am still over here? If more people did a little planning there wouldn't be so many divorces. And that is all we have to do—plan. I could give you all the details, but would take too long to write. Anyway, don't think we're doing things haphazard. The only haphazard thing is when we are going to get married and where.

Well, must sign off, as it is quitting time, and I have to get this off tonight since I won't be in tomorrow.

Love,
Teddy.

Historical Notes: On Saturday, July 28, 1945, a B25 bomber piloted by a veteran of thirty-four bombing missions over Germany crashed in dense fog into the Empire State Building, killing fourteen, including himself, his co-pilot, and a passenger. The air space over New York City was busy that day, and as Lieutenant Colonel William Franklin Smith Jr. was impatient to land, he falsely told officials at La Guardia airport that he had "official business." Air control gave him permission to land, but also warned him that, "At present, we can't see the top of the Empire State Building." Neither could he.

On August 6 and 9, the Japanese cities of Hiroshima and Nagasaki were destroyed by atomic bombs dropped by the United States, killing at least 100,000 civilians outright and many more over time. One of the primary reasons given for the use of the bomb was that it would force Japan to surrender unconditionally. Japan presented its formal document of surrender to the Allied powers on August 15.

August 22/45.

Dear Mom & Dad & Blanche:

Got Blanche's letter of the 10th yesterday. Got a letter from Dorothy Monday, so have got my mail this week.

We all got quite a kick out of Blanche's letter—what a change to shelling peas from her round of cocktail parties and teas! However her descriptions of Toronto take me back to my Ontario days.

I am still up with Mabel, but we get along O.K. and have enough room. Monday night the screw fell out of one of the lens of my glasses, so I am now reduced to wearing my Service ones, and I do mean reduced. However, I took them in to an Optometrist today and he promised them in three or four days.

We had a nice time at the Isle of Wight. Mrs. Salmon greeted me with open arms, and a big kiss. The weather could have been nicer, and it didn't get warm enough to give us courage to go in the sea. Saturday afternoon we window-shopped in the town. Bought a mouse-trap and a kit-bag handle. Walked through Chine and the old village.

Sunday morning we were walking through town and happened to pass a bus station that had a tour going out and coming back at lunch-time, so we went on it. We were gone about 3 hours. Saw several old villages and lots of the country. I would say we saw about quarter of the Island, and stopped for half an hour at that. Sunday afternoon we walked away down the beach and paddled. We left on the 4:40 train, got the 6 o'clock ferry, and a fast train back to London. We got home about 9:30, cooked dinner, did the dishes, did some shining and went to bed. Bert met me for lunch Monday, we had supper at night, and then he had to leave early for camp.

Last night Mabel and I had a domestic evening shining and pressing, since there was C.O.'s parade this morning at 8:15. However, it is only once a week, and we can't kick, since they have cut our working hours a bit.

The weather has been unusually cold—probably September will be hot. I still can't see where August has gone. It seems now as if everybody is just waiting to get home.

Rita just came in all thrilled, because she saw Anthony Eden[53] at noon-hour.

I haven't heard any more from Jack Woods, so I imagine he is on his way home.

Doug is still in the hospital, so I am still in Engineering, struggling with the Winco. He has gone away today, and I am working for the other officers, but taking it easy for a change. The Winco keeps me on the jump. I met one of the other officers I was working for in D.A.S. looking very harassed, and he asked when I was coming back. Just can't get along without me, any of them.

How is Dad these days? How is the crop doing? I suppose you will all be killing yourselves soon, getting it off.

No word yet about going home. I hope we won't have to spend another winter beside a fire-place. People lead me to believe that Ottawa is quite civilized, but all I ask is to be put in a house with Central Heating.

Must sign off now and do some work for dear F/O Kennedy—the lost junior of Engineering.

Lots of love,
Teddy.

August 28/45.

Dear Mom, Dad & Blanche:

Received your letter of August 18th.

I guess with the harvest coming on so fast that I won't get home even to see the tail-end of it. All the fighting men are going home and we have to clean up the dirty details. I am still in Engineering—Doug is out of the

---

[53] Anthony Eden (1897–1977), foreign secretary during the war and successor to Churchill as prime minister of Great Britain in 1955.

hospital, but the M.O. gave him a 48. The Winco nearly had apoplexy—he was mad because Doug took it. That is about how unreasonable he is. I will be glad to get back to the D.A.S. Orderly Room and get a rest.

. . . Did I tell you that I finally saw Mr. Brunker? He brought some magazines around to the house one Saturday afternoon when I happened to be home. . . .

Had a very quiet week. Bert came in Saturday afternoon. Saturday night the four of us went to the dog races at White City Stadium. They have them under the flood-lights now, and it is really nice. When the race is about to start, they turn out all the lights except on the track, and that is all you see— the bright green grass and that ridiculous rabbit and the hounds loping along after it. We saw a record made—Magic Bohemian did 525 yards in 29 seconds. Talk about running! We were all quite flat and hoped to improve our fortunes, so after dropping a little we had to quit.

Last week we got a parcel from Julia (the girl who used to be Mabel's room-mate and went home), so when we came home from the dogs we had Canadian coffee and crackers and cheese. We got to bed in not too bad time and slept in until late Sunday. Mac had to go to work, and Mabel went to church until 12 o'clock. Jim came in from an all-night party, and he and I made breakfast while Bert went out to get some papers. The boys did the dishes while I took a bath. When Mabel got back from church she and Bert and I went down to Hyde Park, we walked a ways, then met Doug and a couple of his cronies, sat and talked to them then decided we had better get home to cook dinner for Mac. He was already home, slightly peeved, and Jim had dinner practically cooked. After sitting around trying to think of some way to spend the evening that wouldn't cost anything, Jim unexpectedly paid back a pound he had borrowed from me, so with that God-send we went to a show. We saw "Isle of Fury" which I swear is the first picture Humphrey Bogart ever made.[54]

. . .

Haven't heard any more from Jack Wood, so guess he must be on his way home.

News is in a sad state here. Aside from one column on the deportment of the Jap envoys and a little they can find out about prisoners, the papers have gone back to such pithy new items as "Have Cats Brains?" and "Ten Points on How to Fertilize Your Garden." The News of the World is a Sunday paper devoted to scandal. On Sunday Bert opened it up and, surprised, said, "What's wrong? Only 6 pages this week." Mac promptly replied, "Oh, all the Canadians have gone home."

---

[54] Humphrey Bogart's first film was *Big City Blues*, in 1932. *Isle of Fury* was made in 1936.

Now that all the P.O.W.'s are back, there are several court martials on for men who collaborated with the enemy. I think it's too bad—you can hardly blame them for wanting to make their lot easier. And the war is won, so you'd think they'd let bygones be bygones. It sure isn't taking England long to make use of the German inventions.

Well, I have kind of run out of news, so will close this and get it in the mail.
Love,
Teddy.

Sept. 5. 45

Dear Mom & Dad & Blanche:

Received letter of August 21 on Saturday.

Haven't done much exciting. Had rather an unexciting domestic week. Bert and a friend were in Friday night. They came to town on an educational tour from camp. They went down the river from Richmond to Hampton Court and beyond, then had some time before the last train back to camp, instead of going back in the truck. He was also in Saturday for the weekend. We had tea and the four of us decided to go to the show early. We only stood in the cue [*sic*] for about half and hour. We enjoyed it though—"The Affairs of Susan." Only we knew all along she would marry her husband again. We got home about 10, had sardines on toast, sat and listened to the radio, and went to bed. Sunday morning we had breakfast about 11, and Mabel and Mac went to church. Jim and I did the dishes and cleaned up. Then I took a bath and dressed, and by that time Mabel and Mac were back. We went out to Hyde Park, and as soon as we got out it turned cold and windy. We got home about 4, and set about cooking dinner. The amount of stuff we cooked was immense and I thought we would never get rid of it, but we did. We had mutton chops, corn on the cob (at 1 shilling per cob), wax beans, chips and celery. Quite a mixture!

After the dishes were done, we had ambition for nothing. Bert had Monday off (somebody said it was Labour Day, and I said it sure was). He met me for lunch at noon, I collected two weeks' laundry and he took it home for me. We ate at Bertorelli's at night, and he had to leave early.

. . .

So far, September has been just as cold as August, and rainy into the bargain. We had C.O.'s parade this morning, and my hands haven't got warm yet. Just a gesture of defiance we made tea, although we are not supposed to waste time in the morning making it.

Some things are improving here. We can get tooth-paste, Cutex hand cream, Listerine, and even Eno's Fruit Salts. Food gets no better, although there is fruit and vegetables now. The radio is pretty grim now. They used to have records of Jack Benny, Fred Allan, and Charlie McArthy, but now have decided to be entirely independent. They have two programs—The Home

Service and the Light program, and those are the only two you can get in London. You know they have no commercial programs, and the talent the B.B.C. sponsors must all be friends of the directors.

At last they have given us a definite policy with regard to repat. They have asked for volunteers to forego the privilege of repat by number and stay until they don't need them anymore. They don't plan on getting enough volunteers, and intend to make the people with the highest numbers stay past their time—the highest numbers are the ones with the least repat priority. The married women they are sending right away—to be home by October 1st. Other than that, they are repatting by straight numbers. That means that they won't be able to start until at least October, since the 150 married women will be all they can cope with at once. By the time my group comes up it will be late November or December, probably.

The Army has slowed down, and Bert doesn't expect his number to come until around then. Because of this slow-down, we thought we might get married, but I found out that once you are married and it reaches your documents, they ship you right home. So if we got married, say this month, by the time the machinery moved I would be sent home some time in October, and Bert wouldn't be coming for maybe two months. It's a sorry mess the Service makes of things. If Bert should get sent soon, it would be wise for us to get married to get me home. I am not going to volunteer to stay. I will either get married or wait my turn by number—it isn't the highest, anyway. I suppose there is no use asking you what you think—I note you have carefully and coldly avoided all mention of it.

I thought I would be getting a nice rest coming back to D.A.S., but there seem to be a few kids away, and this morning is the first time I have had to write a letter this week, and then I had to interrupt it to do a job.

I read "Forever Amber" last week. Quite a feat, and I still haven't decided whether it was worth it.

Oh, my gosh, I almost forgot to tell you—I got a parcel last week, with butter and shortbread and spam. It was very welcome, thank you. I couldn't see the date—the post-mark was blurred. I also got one Saturday from Aunt Maude, with T.P., soap and Kleenex and chocolate bars.

Must sign off, now.
Lots of love,
Teddy.

Forever Amber—the first really explicit novel. Somebody had loaned Mabel a copy, just for the weekend. We were both trying to read it, so it took every minute. Mac and Bert got disgusted trying to get us out, so climbed out a neighbouring window onto our window ledge. This scared us enough to leave the book.

September 18, 1945.

Dear Mom, Dad & Blanche:

Got your two letters last week, and got Blanche's yesterday. Suppose harvest is going full tilt now. Hope it turns out better than it looks.

Blanche didn't say why she didn't go to work at Simpson's. . . .

I am writing this at noon-hour, and there is an English Army band outside playing selections from the Mikado, and they sound very good. A couple of weeks ago Mabel and I saw a notice board outside Albert Hall announcing that Francis Cassel was giving a concert. We like the list of songs he (or she) was going to do, so got tickets for it. It is next Wednesday. We don't even know what this character plays—violin, piano, or piccolo. I will let you know when I hear it whether it was worth 7 and 6—pardon me, 7 shillings, 6 pence. . . .

I was detailed for a Church Parade last Sunday, but told the Major I refused to go, since I was supposed to be on a 48, and had planned going to the Isle of Wight for a long time, and Bert only got a 48 once every 3 months. Much to my surprise, he phoned the discip. section, and got me off the parade.

Mabel and Mac had been at Torquay on leave all week, and we were going to meet them at Shanklin. Bert and I left here at 10:45 and arrived at Shanklin about 2:30. Of course Mrs. Salmon had to make us tea, and then as her girl was away for the weekend, and she said she didn't like to ask any of the rest of the people who were staying there, we did her shopping. After that we walked around the town, met a couple of trains, and finally went back for supper at 6:30. After that we decided to go to the coach station and try to get on a tour.

The only one that was running was a mystery tour, so we decided to try that. It was starting to get dark when we left. We went South, through Ventnor and the Undercliff. It was a terrible zig-zag road, and dark with trees on both sides. We passed Lloyd's tower, where all ships coming through the Channel have to report, and the strongest light-house on the English Coast—15 million candle-power—which can be seen in France and the southernmost tip of the Island. We stopped at an old rum-runners or smugglers inn—the Buddle Inn. It was cute—low ceilings, black beams, rough stone floor, and pewter mugs hanging from the beams, and a huge open fire-place. We drove on to Blackgang Chine, which was closed, so I still don't know what it is. So we went to another old pub—The Star. This was also old, but bigger, and not as cute as the Buddle. Besides, a gang of shipyard workers were having a party there. They were having an impromptu concert, too. There were only a couple of women, and of course they tried to get the girls from the bus-load to dance. No go, so they danced with each other. The funniest sight was two old men, who were old enough to totter anyway, dancing together. Finally the bus-driver got us all away. A couple of the men wanted Bert and I to stay, and to drive us home afterwards. I bet not one of them got home themselves. As it was, we made it by about 10. Mac and Mabel had arrived, so after gabbing for about an hour and a half, we finally got to bed.

Sunday morning we went out for a walk. It had rained and was quite wet. We found a rutty track that led up a big hill, that is just back of the town. We got up it, and the boys were satisfied to go that far, but Mabel and I insisted on going up the last little steep bit to the top. With the help of cow tracks we got up in spite of the wet grass, and almost had to slide on our fanny to get down again, thoroughly wet. The boys were thoroughly disgusted. We just got back in time for dinner. After that, we went down and sat on the sand in the cold wind. We took off our shoes and paddled just to get a picture. By the time we had tea and packed and dressed, it was time to get the train. We got a boat just before 6, so got the fast 7 o'clock train. Bert came to Havant on it, but had to change to a slow one that stopped at Liss, so he could get over to camp from there.

Last night, needless to say, I went to bed at 9:30. Must do a huge laundry tonight—still doing my own, since I got some new spots over the weekend. The ones I have get better alright, if no more would come I'd be alright. Tomorrow night there is a H.Q. dance—don't know if I'll go. I also want to see Betty Hutton in "Incendiary Blond" which is on at our local cinema this week.

Must do some work now, so will sign off.

Lots of love,

Teddy.

P.S. Bert expects to be in repat depot by the end of October, but I still don't know. My guess is still Xmas.

On our last weekend at Shanklin, our hostess took us out to a pub to meet her friends. Somehow, at the end of the evening, about eight of us were whooping along a path at the top of a cliff, doing a Rockette-style march to the tune of a loud "Knees Up Mother Brown," a well-known music hall song that is thankfully forgotten.

September 25/45.

Dear Mom & Dad & Blanche:

Received your letter of Sept. 11 on Saturday. Hope you have got more crop in since then.

I'm getting darned fed up not knowing what they are going to do with us. I don't think anybody knows, and nobody takes any action. I still hope to make it for Christmas.

It has been wet here. Hardly any of the farmers got all their crops in and had to plough it back into the ground in order to get the next crop in. Yesterday and today have been bright and crisp, just like Fall.

People who volunteered to stay over here as long as they are needed are going to be let go to Paris for leave. Two plane seats a week are reserved for

D.A.S. Sure wish I could wangle a trip over for eight days. There are very few in the Directorate who volunteered.

Last week there was an article in one of the Sunday papers about the Canadians, and it started like this: "The captains and kings depart, the tumult and shouting dies—the Canadians are going home." Kipling (or was it Tennyson?) would turn over in his grave.[55]

Didn't do much last week. Went to bed early every night. Bert came Saturday afternoon. Mabel and I weren't in yet, and of course the boys were disgusted.

We had decided to go to a fashion show on Piccadilly when we came out of work. This exhibition is of French designers and came over from Paris. They are all on dolls about 2? ft. high to save material. There sure are some lovely clothes. Some of the designing is very intricate. Nearly all the afternoon dresses have enormous shoulders and yards of skirt. There was a suit just about like that old blue one of Blanche's, only in brown, and the jacket was longer. There was very little fur—it is terribly expensive here. There were quite a few printed silk afternoon dresses and some cotton evening dresses. There was a black net evening dress with full skirt like Blanche's, but it had solid rows of net frills, and each black net frill had a white lace frill under it. Also the top was very fussy. There were very few dresses bare at the top. We sure enjoyed looking at the clothes, anyway. We gave vent to our want of luxury by buying some pine bath essence.

Well, anyway, as we were coming up Holland Road, the boys were coming out of the house, disgusted with waiting, on their way to the pub. We sat around and gabbed, made tea, and finally went out for supper. We then took bus and tube to Piccadilly, just to look at the crowds. We walked along to Leicester Square, then down to Trafalgar Square. They have an exhibition on there, but it was not lighted, so we looked at a frog-man, German Mk. IV tank, anti-aircraft gun and 88 gun, and a V2 in the dark. Then we went into an old pub on the Strand—The Coal Hole, and got a bus straight home from there. We had tea again and got to bed, all worn out.

Sunday morning Mabel and Mac got up to go to church and, get this, so did Bert and I. We went to our old favorite—at least we have been there before, twice—St. John's Presbyterian. I know how Blanche felt, trying to find a church to go to where there is no U.C. Besides, Bert is a Presbyterian. The minister of St. John's is an American Scotchman. Mabel and Mac had got home before us, and had washed the breakfast dishes. We had sandwiches, then went out to Hyde Park between rain showers to take some pictures of the German aircraft exhibition there. The usual row of orators was at work. One poor guy on a soap-box was getting the works from a couple of New Zealand

---

[55] Actually, it is Kipling, from his hymn, "Recessional," which he wrote in honour of Queen Victoria's Diamond Jubilee in 1897.

sailors. There was one Socialist, one Communist, two religious speakers, and two or three people just talking to hear themselves. We got on the bus for home just as another shower started. Mabel and Mac cooked dinner, and we washed the dishes.

Yesterday morning I was as sick as a dog, and went back to bed instead of going to work. I had a kind of summer flu again, and thought I'd die before the doctor came. He gave me some codeine pills, which deadened my stomach ache when I kept taking them, and I slept nearly all day. This morning I felt better and came to work. I am back in D.A.S. now, Pauline being back from leave.

Guess I had better stop now and get to work, which as far as I can see now consists of cleaning up my desk. I can't think of anything more to say now, anyway.

Love,
Teddy.

October 1/45.

Dear Mom, Dad & Blanche:

Received letter of Sept. 16, today. . . .

I managed to make the supernumerary list, but I'm afraid it won't help much. We are surplus at H.Q., but there is no place to send us anyway, so we will probably stay here. I understand shipping is to be cut sharply after this month—most of the boats have to put in for repairs, so if we don't go this month it might be around New Year's. However, you never know what the Air Force is going to do. The only possible way I could get home right away would be to get married, and there is too much red tape to that over here.

Listen, you stupid drip, Blanche, even I know when a muffin batter has enough flour in it, and that is clearly what was wrong with your muffins. You should see the dinners we cook every Sunday—we use almost a whole week's rations.

Can't say I like my birthday present delayed—it will be just like your birthday in Washington. Probably it will end up combined with my Christmas present and be something for a house. My heart's desire now winter is coming is an elastic girdle. I haven't one at all.

. . .

Last week was quite quiet. We enjoyed the concert in Albert Hall. Francis Cassel turned out to be very good, and he played stuff that was listen-able. He did a Chopin group, but compensated for it by doing a Liszt group.

Thursday night Acton Army Records had a dance. Mac borrowed someone else's building pass and got a ticket for Bert, who managed to get in. They weren't busy, so he got off until Friday noon, which meant he could stay the night. It was quite a good dance—not as many drunks as the Air Force dances, and they had our good Air Force dance orchestra.

I just received your birthday card—pretty fast, wasn't it? Thanks very much—all the kids think it is cute. One of the girls who got married two weeks ago just got her posting to repat depot—they didn't lose much time.

Well, to continue. Friday night I did my washing. Bert came in Saturday afternoon. We had just come in and Mac had an address to look for rooms, so we went right out again, and Bert and Vic (an R.A.F. chap we met at Killarney) were waiting for us. We had tea, then went out again. Then again Sunday morning, and Sunday afternoon to tell some people we would take a room we saw. They own several houses all together, so Mac and Jim are taking that double room, and we expect to get in there soon. We haven't given our notice, but Mrs. MacLean knows darned well we are moving. Needless to say, after all that we were fatigued, and didn't do much else.

To-night we are having supper and a shower at the Canadian Y.W.C.A. for Kay Lewis's (a girl in this Orderly Room) sister.

I have been putting off my leave, as they have started letting us take leave in Paris. So far only Permanent Force and people who have volunteered to stay here as long as they are needed can go, but I think it might be broadened. D.A.S. are allowed two plane seats a week, so I have hopes. If it doesn't look hopeful by the end of this month, I probably will go to Cornwall or Isle of Wight. Needless to say, Major Warner went this week with the first lot, then he is going home the week after.

Well, there isn't anything else to say—news is scarce, and I must quit anyway to do a signal.

Love,
Teddy.

Nov. 28

Dear Folks:

Well, it won't be long now—Sunday is getting closer. We have been having a fairly easy time—having roll call twice a day and doing nothing else except eat. Of course walking around (just got some ink[56]) tires you out since the town is all hills.

Thursday

Got Mom's letter yesterday and Blanche's today. The job situation doesn't sound so hot—maybe I'd better stay in the Service.

We are going on the boat Saturday. All my odds and ends are cleared up. My kit bags finally came, and though they miss the Lizzie, may make the Mauritania on the 6th. The Lizzie is going to try to beat the record this crossing. She can't go too fast to suit me. I'm not very happy about that train trip, but I guess I'm as good a traveller as usual.

[56] Start of letter written in pencil.

Glad Grandpa is better—he'll probably keep on improving now.

I bought the cutest pewter beer-mug and teapot. They are adorable and I couldn't resist them. Bert is going to send them to me. He has a chance of driving in a convoy of trucks going to North West Europe. Don't know yet if he took it.

There doesn't seem to be much to say. Depends on the time the boat makes when I arrive. We have to spend about 5 hours at Lachine, getting paid, etc.

Just have a hot bath and bed for me, and let me die. I've only been warm about once since we came down here.

Be seeing you.

Love

Teddy.

Epilogue

I was shipped home in December. The voyage home on the Queen Elizabeth *was not exactly as we expected, but it <u>was</u> on the* Queen Elizabeth, *with 10,000 troops.*

We received only two meals a day on the Queen Elizabeth, *but no complaints because they were good, with white bread. We landed in New Jersey, were loaded off onto twenty-five trains, and were one whole day late arriving in Vancouver—partly due to fish-trains' right-of-way. But I was home in time for Christmas.*

While I was in England, all of my family, in bits, moved to British Columbia (but I found them anyway). So, when the troop train arrived in Vancouver, it was only family I was returning to, not home.

Bert, however, was not repatted until the end of March 1946. As soon as he arrived in Ottawa, where his family lived, he flew out to Vancouver, and we were married on April 15, on a week's notice. Bert had re-enlisted in the Regular Army and had to report to work. We then returned to Ottawa and, together with our two sons, served postings in Gagetown, New Brunswick, Japan, Belgium, and Ottawa. After retiring from the Army, he worked for the Township of Nepean and County of Carleton school boards, keeping track of equipment. He passed away in 1971.

I worked in the library of National Health and Welfare until 1974, the two sons growing up apace and starting work, getting married and all. I also did much volunteer political work, and have put in many years with the Royal Canadian Legion and Good Companions, a seniors' group in Ottawa.

My sister Blanche, the receiver of these accounts along with my mother and father, lives in Kelowna, British Columbia, a happy ninety-three year old.

So, looking back on this period of my life from a sixty-year-long viewpoint, I am essentially satisfied.

During the war years, I had experiences that tested my understanding and tolerance. I met many people and found out how people differ. As well as this being a benefit to me, I feel that I did do work that was a cog, no matter how small, in Canada's war effort.

To order more copies of

Letters
from London
1944–45

Contact:
**GENERAL STORE
PUBLISHING HOUSE**
499 O'Brien Road, Box 415
Renfrew, Ontario Canada K7V 4A6
Telephone: 1-800-465-6072
Fax: (613) 432-7184
www.gsph.com

VISA and MASTERCARD accepted.